DATE

Opportunity
KNOCKS

Opportunity KNOCKS

American Economic Policy After Gorbachev

ROBERT A. SOLO

M. E. SHARPE, INC.
Armonk, New York • London, England

Library of Congress Cataloging-in-Publication Data

Solo, Robert A.
    Opportunity knocks: American economic policy after Gorbachev / Robert A. Solo.
        p.   cm.
      ISBN 0-87332-774-8 (cloth)
        1. Economic conversion—United States.   2. United States—Economic
policy—1981– 3. United States—Economic conditions—1981–
4. United States—Commerce.   I. Title.
HC110.D4S55   1991
338.973—dc20

Printed in the United States of America

BB   10   9   8   7   6   5   4   3   2   1   90–46944
                                                                        CIP

To

Kenneth Ewart Boulding

Great man, great friend

Table of Contents

Prologue
Gorbachev's Gift   3

PART 1   HOW CAN WE HAVE FULL EMPLOYMENT
         AND PRICE STABILITY?

Memorandum   10
  1 Policy Revisited   11
  2 Questions   19
  3 Answers   29

PART 2   THE QUESTION OF POLITICAL COMPETENCE:
         MITI AND AIM

Memorandum   42
  4 MITI and the Instrumentality of Economic Reform   43
  5 AIM   59

PART 3   HOW CAN WE REGAIN TECHNOLOGICAL
         PREEMINENCE AND ACCELERATE THE
         RISE OF AMERICAN INDUSTRIAL
         PRODUCTIVITY?

Memorandum   66
  6 Losing the Race   69
  7 Some Elements of the System   73
  8 Decline of the American System   79

9   Policies   99
10   Crisis   113

PART 4   HOW CAN WE ACHIEVE BALANCED
         INTERNATIONAL TRADE?

    Memorandum   128
11   The Benefits of Trade   129
12   The Continuum of Imbalance   135
13   Finding Balance   141
14   The International Flight of Cash Balances   147

PART 5   IS THERE A PREFERRED ALTERNATIVE
         TO A WORLD SYSTEM OF INTERNATIONAL
         FREE TRADE?

    Memorandum   154
15   Options and Choices   155
16   Comparison and Contrast   159
17   Policy Implications   163

PART 6   WHAT POLICY CAN CONFRONT THE
         DEPLETION AND ULTIMATE EXHAUSTION
         OF A CRITICAL NATURAL RESOURCE?

    Memorandum   174
18   Perceptions   177
19   Problems and Policies   181
20   Survival   191

Index   199

PROLOGUE

GORBACHEV'S GIFT

Prologue

Gorbachev's Gift

It was my original intention in this chapter to project alternative scenarios for our future, one a doomsday scenario, and the other, one of hope and beneficence. Suddenly, our future is no longer in the distance. It is here and now, within our hands. The chance for a future is within our grasp.

For nearly half a century, we have armed ourselves to the teeth, spent our substance, and gone into industrial decline trying to organize and control the world in a fight against the threat to American security of Russian communism. Into the maw of military spending we poured the resources that could have renewed and renewed again the whole of our industrial structure. Into its maw we poured the energy and creativity of the great part of the nation's trained scientists and research engineers, who would otherwise have spearheaded the advance of industrial technology. Instead, they devised the weapons of death.

What was this threat that so troubled and mobilized our people, that obsessed the CIA, the Department of State, our presidents, beginning with that mean-faced man from Missouri, and followed by the rest, one after the other, like stand-up comics taking their turn on the stage of power? It was the threat, not of the Russian people, but of communism, COMMUNISM, conceived as a gigantic, world-embracing conspiracy to foment revolution, subvert capitalism (and democracy), and one way or another, take over the good old United States of America. Of course, the threat was not just of communism as a diabolic but disembodied theory, but of a communism that had captured and controlled the power of Russia; a power that, its back against the wall, had destroyed the mighty Nazi war machine, and in so doing, had

3

saved our collective hides. The threat was of Russian communism.

Was there ever really a threat, a real threat to American security? I never believed there was. Soviet performance in the war against Afghanistan, and the now exposed realities of what had been the Warsaw Pact and of an empire held together with paper and paste, all suggest that I was right in my heresy. Be that as it may. It was that idea of Russian communism as gigantic conspiracy and viable threat that must account for, explain, rationalize, justify, our enormous military expenditures, our wars in Korea and Vietnam, our installation of right wing dictators in Latin America and elsewhere, our financing of the contras in Nicaragua, the massive subventions to Salvador, Pakistan, Israel, Egypt, and Iran under the Shah, our interventions in Afghanistan and Angola, and even our support for the murderous Pol Pot and the Khmer Rouge. This was all in the name of protecting American security, not from the government of Angola, not from the Vietcong, not from the Sandinistas, not from tiny Grenada; all these mattered only as the alleged tools of Moscow. The only threat was of Russian communism.

Whatever might once have been the reality, even the shadow of that threat is now entirely vanished. The specter is gone. Communism is dead and buried. Communism is dead in Russia. The Warsaw Pact has blown away. The states of Eastern Europe are tumbling over each other to get on the capitalist bandwagon. And East Germany is to be absorbed into West Germany. For the first time in the century, there is no plausible threat anywhere in the world to American security, nor is there any on the horizon; save, of course, for the sheer existence of the atomic stockpiles.

We owe it all to Gorbachev. That is Gorbachev's great gift to us. He has junked the old system of a centralized, politically directed society and economy. He has put his faith in private initiative and human reason; in the people and in democracy; in the effort to transform the empire into a federation of autonomous democratic republics. In so doing, he has exposed his country to the tumultuous and profoundly dangerous forces of transition. The economy is in shambles. The polity faces the threat of total disintegration; yet Gorbachev strives to hold his course.

At this moment, for this moment, the world is in our hands; in President Bush's hands; in the hands of our leadership. We know that Gorbachev will follow us in any reasonable plan for mutual demilitari-

zation and disarmament. It is only for us to propose. In any case, there
has ceased to be any reason or rationale for massive armament and
militarization in the United States, or for the policy of supporting the
most vile and vicious oligarchies, juntas, and dictatorships, as long as
they are professed anticommunists. There is no longer any reason to be
concerned about Salvador and Nicaragua. The old justification for
massive subvention and intervention is gone. We could as well be rid
of the CIA. As for NATO? It is a military alliance, poised to defend
against what? Ready to release its deadly weaponry in an attack against
whom? NATO, now purposeless, becomes a bastion of militarism, a
dangerous anachronism, planted in the heart of Europe.

What a glorious opportunity for us; an open field for greatness of
vision. It is in our hands to rid the world of the threat of nuclear
devastation, now. It is in our hands to release enormous resources from
military bondage throughout the world, and to lead the world in using
those resources to produce the means and instruments of renewal and
life. Never in living memory has there been such an opportunity to
capture the good future as is now given to us. That is Gorbachev's gift.
What will we do with it?

Alas, the habits of mind shaped during the generations of the cold
war are not so easy to change. What we observe, what we know as
fact, seeps only slowly into the recesses of the mind to reach our
awareness, to transform our mode of perception. President Bush resists
the siren call of peace. Instead of joining with Gorbachev to bring an
end to the nuclear nightmare; instead of joining with Gorbachev in
ridding the world of the heavy burden of arms; instead of walking
together with him toward the future of peace and plenty; our president
squeezes Gorbachev, whose back is against the wall, squeezes him like
a shyster for any and every concession, for unbalanced reductions in
arms to increase our now pointless military advantage. He travels the
country to promote fear and protect military spending. Under popular
and congressional pressure, the secretary of defense concedes a peace
dividend of two percent. Two percent! Then, in a ploy to dampen
congressional enthusiasm for cuts in military spending, he would eliminate not weapons, but military bases in congressional districts. Alas
for the lack of courage. Alas for the lack of vision.

Soviet communism has ceased to be a threat to the United States or
to anyone. But out of its demise arises a spate of militant, warring
nationalisms in fanatic pursuit of vengeance, glory, or domination. We

see it already in the massacres and the blind and bloody strife of Hungarians and Romanians, Bulgarians and Turks, Armenians and Azerbaijanies, and Serbs and Albanians, in a movement that carries Central and Eastern Europe back toward a balkanization like unto the tinder box of the First World War. And what of the reunion of the two Germanys, fused by the force of nationalism into a power already destined to dominate Western Europe?

One hopes, along with so many Germans, that their enormously rich and powerful country will become a bastion of stability and a force for peace. Yet, given the cultural proclivities and traditions of Germany, and the experience of two world wars and of Hitler and the Nazis, the possibility of a return of rampant and ferocious German nationalism, coupled with German military genius, cannot be overlooked.

Rather than encouraging the demand of a great many Germans for a neutral and peaceful Germany, rid of nuclear implantations and rid of arms and armies, and secure in its industrial might and economic well-being, our president and his people, and Margaret Thatcher and hers, insist on bringing the united Germany into NATO (in a military alliance against what? against whom?), allegedly to check and control any resurgence of militarism in Germany. Can it be believed? German militarism is to be kept in check, the power of the new giant to be controlled, by seeding it with the militancy of the Alliance? A militant Germany will not be dominated and controlled by NATO: It will dominate and control NATO.

And if the genie that Hitler once conjured up should rise again, then what force would there be in Europe to balance it? There could be none other than the strong, democratic federation of autonomous republics that Gorbachev seeks. That is our stake in his success.

The game has only begun. President Bush will not for long withstand the force of reason and the pressures of the members of Congress for balanced budgets and for benefits to their constituents. The massive cut in military spending will certainly come, bringing in its train (as will be demonstrated in chapter 10) grave problems for economic policy and planning.

Here we may indulge in some futurism, projecting from this point a scenario of survival and hope.

Suppose the United States and the Soviet Union, in order to rid the world of the nuclear nightmare, agreed to destroy all their nuclear weapons and the facilities with which to produce them. Such an agreement is today within our grasp. But to achieve our objective of a world safe from nuclear attack, we must take into account the nuclear weaponry in the hands of other nations that possess or that could produce them. Given an agreement between the Soviet Union and the United States, it is to be expected that those other nations, for the sake of their own survival, and pressed by the Americans, the Russians, and the rest of the world, would enter into the same agreement.

The agreement must be enforced by joint American and Russian inspection teams and the force of American and Russian arms at first, but ultimately through the formation of a transnational agency to ensure the elimination of all nuclear arsenals, to stop the production of and traffic in all nuclear arms, and to monitor the production and use of all nuclear materials. This agency would be transnational rather than international in that it would not represent the nations and facilitate relations between them, but would stand outside the nations and serve them all. Such agencies already exist (for example, the World Bank and the International Monetary Fund), representing a step in the formation of a transnational state.

In order to survive, the agency, charged with the enforcement of the nuclear arms agreement, would have to cultivate, enlist, and rely upon the support of the people of all nations, and the peoples of the world would give their support when they came to understand that their survival depended on the agency's performance of its task. The competencies that agency would, of necessity, develop, the technologies it would master, the worldwide electronic network for automated observation and data interpretation it would put in place, would be perfectly suited to another critical task of monitoring and control. And the agency, taking another step in our scenario of hope and survival, would undertake to monitor and protect the endangered *commons* of the globe: the oceans and the seas, their ecologies and aquatic life, the atmosphere and the biosphere—all the great open systems essential to the life of all peoples that escape the reach of any one nation.

A part of the research and development capabilities released through disarmament would be organized transnationally to deal with these endangered commons of the globe in the development of benign, non-polluting technologies appropriate to a time of resource closure.

Within specified limits and in the performance of delegated tasks, the transnational agency would become the sovereign instrument of an incipient transnational state, and its acceptance and success would open the world of nations to further transformation. Given that the transnational agency might be challenged as having exceeded its delegated powers, or as having failed to fulfill its assigned responsibilities, judgment would have to be made, and remedies imposed, by reference to a charter delegating the agency's tasks, responsibilities, and powers. Ipso facto, that charter would have the character of a written constitution, and the resolution of disputes concerning it would require judicial determination. Necessarily, a transnational court would be established with powers analogous to the Supreme Court of the United States in interpreting obligations, powers, and constraints under the charter.

Thus, we will have crossed the threshold of survival, and established there the solid groundwork for a new era in human history. Such is the vision. Such is the potential. Such might be the goal.

In asking questions that must be asked, and in offering answers that might be given, the chapters that follow will stake out a path through the open door of opportunity, into our economic future.

February 17, 1990
East Lansing, Michigan

PART 1

HOW CAN WE HAVE FULL EMPLOYMENT AND PRICE STABILITY?

Memorandum

To: Reader
From: Author
Subject: Depression, mass unemployment, and inflation

1. The goal is full employment and stable prices. Can we achieve that goal? What stands in the way of our achieving it?

2. To find answers we must confront a host of related questions.

What happened to Keynesian full employment policy, showpiece of earlier decades?

What is the character of the stagflation that brought Keynesian full employment policy down? What should be done to deal with stagflation?

3. We will argue that it is possible to achieve full employment without inflation, but only through public/corporate co-participation in the formation of price policy for the corporate industrial sector of the economy.

4. We will propose a more responsible, more effective, less costly system for the public management of aggregate expenditure.

5. The great social cost of the Keynesian system for the management of aggregate expenditure has been in the use of deficit finance as an instrument for generating additions to the spending stream, with the rising obligation to pay interest on a public debt as its consequence. We propose an alternative instrument to serve the same purpose without incurring the burden of that obligation.

1 • Policy Revisited

I will not take up the cudgels with Dr. Pangloss to prove all is not well with the workings of the free market. That there are problems, I take as given. My purpose is to propose the means of solving them. For that I must first explain the nature of those problems and review the history of our experience concerning them. In this we will be covering familiar ground, and reviewing theories in terms as simple and as abbreviated as is compatible with the arguments we intend to make and the policies we will propose. Here the focal problem is that of depression and inflation. Our objective is a workable policy for full employment and price stability.

Depression and the Welfare State

Karl Marx predicted that a crisis of mass unemployment, becoming increasingly severe, would eventually bring capitalism down. He was right. The Great Depression of the thirties brought the old system of world capitalism down, but the revolutionary changes that followed were quite different from what Marx had envisaged. Out of that depression came the welfare state, providing buffers against the depredations of old age, sickness, and disemployment. What gave this new welfare state its dynamic value was a policy for full employment and price stability associated with the term "Keynesianism."

The essence of Keynesianism is simple, and its truth would seem obvious to the naked eye. Mass unemployment exists because consumers are not buying enough and/or firms are not investing enough. The total purchasing by individuals and businesses is not sufficient; hence, mass unemployment can be eliminated by increasing this aggregate demand. For generations, the despised "underconsumptionists" had been insisting on this, and for generations, their truth was ignored. Why? Because in the prevailing image of the economy as it had been developed by neoclassical economics, a sustained condition of mass unemployment simply could not exist in a free market economy.

The Neoclassical Mode of Thought

The neoclassical mode of thought was (and is) dominated by the image of an economy where an autonomous, free-moving price clears all markets, controls the allocation of resources, and determines the pattern of production and consumption. As perceived by neoclassical economics, the autonomy of free-moving price is the control mechanism and the sine qua non of the economy. An analogue to this model is found in some agricultural markets. The farmer harvests his crop. He brings it to market, and has no option but to sell it at whatever happens to be the market price. If demand has shifted away from his crop to other kinds of consumer expenditure, then the price he receives will be lower, and he will be poorer than he was before. Conversely, he receives a higher price for his product when consumer purchasing shifts away from other things to a greater demand for his crop.

If, in such an economy, rather than a shift in demand between products, there is a simultaneous decline in the demand for all products, that is, a decline in aggregate demand, then prices and wages would decline across the board. The prices our farmer would have to pay for what he purchased would be lower by about as much as the price he received for what he sold. In real terms, he would be no better and no worse off than he was before; nor would the decline in the price level induce him to work less or produce less or hire fewer workers than he did before.

In this form of economy, random changes in aggregate demand produce rapid movements up or down in the price level, but there would be no underconsumption, no overproduction, and no disemployment. The real terms of trade, good for good, would be essentially unaffected.

None of us can bring a system so vast and complex as the nation's economy within the scope of individual observation. Perforce we conceive and comprehend what we have been taught to conceive and comprehend. What we see of reality is filtered through an acquired prism of perception. In the 1930s, it was via the neoclassical mode of thought that economists conceived and comprehended the operation of the actual economy, and for that reason, they denied the possibility of sustained mass unemployment even as that phenomenon was bringing the whole social fabric down.

The Roots of Monetary Policy

The neoclassical model appropriately describes the operation of an agricultural economy such as existed in preindustrial Europe or in early nineteenth-century America. Depressions generating mass unemployment were unknown, but sharp up-and-down movements of the price level traumatized contractual and especially borrower-lender relationships, producing bank failures and panics that threatened the integrity of the financial system.

To ameliorate this problem, central banks, empowered to issue currency, were created, and monetary policy was born. The federal reserve system for the United States was a latecomer to the international circle of central banks. In the American case, the Federal Reserve Board stood ready to issue federal reserve notes, in exchange for the mortgages and other secured assets held by commercial banks. This enabled commercial banks to meet the demand for cash in times of panic by making liquid their otherwise frozen assets.

The central bank and the monetary policy that it employed, devised in preindustrial capitalism, would later be used in the effort to cope with depression and mass unemployment.

Keynesian Full Employment Policy

The economist's and the policymaker's commitment to neoclassical thought buckled under the enormous and sustained catastrophe of the Great Depression of the 1930s. In spite of the doomsaying of the sages, government after government embarked on ad hoc efforts to offset the collapse of aggregate demand. John Maynard Keynes, Britain's most distinguished economist, speaking from the very center of the political establishment, offered an alternative image of the economy wherein, it seemed, economists could embrace a positive policy designed to achieve full employment through the public management of aggregate (private plus public) spending, without abandoning their traditional free market paradigm.

What Keynes offered can be explained with the metaphor of an econosphere held afloat by the pressure of aggregate spending. If the pressure of aggregate spending is too great it rises skyward into the ether of inflation like a great balloon. If the pressure of aggregate spending is insufficient, it sinks into the mire of depression and mass unemployment. It becomes the task of the state to maintain the pressure of aggregate spending at the level where the econosphere floats evenly, with employment full and price unchanging. The role of the state had only to do with maintaining the external pressures of aggregate spending. Within the econosphere, the free movement of price was exactly as described by neoclassical theory. Thus was created a dual economics: macro for the up-and-down swings of the econosphere; micro for the internal operation of the economy.

Unconventional Wisdom Forgotten

Keynes's famous *General Theory* is an example of obscure writing and brilliant, revolutionary thinking that leapt over the deep gullies of conventional thought to a new and broad plain of perception. Some of Keynes's truths were not noticed or understood when he first articulated them. Others, integral to his system, were forgotten as Keynes faded and as the prevailing perception moved back into the neoclassical mold. Here we will recall a few of those truths, for they have a part to play in our argument.

Increased saving, in the sense of individuals spending less of their current income in order to put money ''in the bank,'' does not increase the quantity of money in commercial banks, nor does it increase the potential of commercial banks to lend. All it does is reduce aggregate demand. Should every individual in the community cease to spend anything of their current income in order to save everything they earn to put it all in the bank, not an iota would be added to the supply side of the lending-borrowing equation, while the demand side of that equation (along with current revenues and national income) would be reduced to zero.

An increase in real savings that add to the real assets in individual or corporate possession is brought about not by the decision of consumers to spend less and put the saved money into the bank, but only by the decisions of business to spend more on such things as new plant and equipment or on research and development. Consumer saving in the sense of consumer nonspending is important for growth only when it is necessary to free resources required to accommodate a rising rate of real business investment, while keeping aggregate expenditure constant.

The Golden Age

At the end of World War II, every major capitalist nation was committed to the Keynesian approach. With varying degrees of sophistication they managed their level of aggregate demand. The favored instrument was fiscal policy, with government offsetting too much or too little private sector spending by taxing more than it spent, or spending more than it taxed.

The postwar decades through the 1960s were an absolutely golden age for western capitalism. The rate of growth was unparalleled, with unemployment low and prices stable. In the fifties and the sixties each decade saw a rise in the real income of the American family of approximately 36 percent even though during those years, real growth in the United States was lower, and American rates of unemployment were higher than in other major industrialized countries.

In the 1970s, the rate of growth declined. For that whole decade, the real income of the American family increased by only 6.7 percent. In 1980, growth ceased altogether, and the real income of the American family decreased by 5.5 percent.

Stagflation and the Keynesian Demise

The 1970s brought a particular and peculiar kind of inflation; particular and peculiar because as prices went up, so did unemployment. This stagflation was not in line with Keynesian expectations. In the Keynesian paradigm, inflation was the converse and opposite of unemployment. Keynesian policy of increasing spending to offset unemployment and reducing spending to offset inflation was held at a standstill. If, to check inflation, aggregate expenditure was decreased, the rise in unemployment would accelerate. If in order to offset the high and rising unemployment aggregate expenditure was increased, the rate of inflation would be accelerated. By the end of the 1970s, kicked off by OPEC's deliberated increase in the price of oil, inflation was rampant. Keynesian expenditure management was considered unworkable.

Ex-Keynesians rejoined the neoclassical orthodoxy, celebrating the old-fashioned virtues of sound finance and balanced budgets, demanding a return to the policies of laissez-faire.

The Return to Laissez-faire

When Jimmy Carter was president, welfare policies were sharply reversed. The goal of full employment was abandoned. There was a new faith in the free market, uncorrupted by government regulation. This dismemberment of the activist state accelerated under President Reagan. The same occurred in France, in England, and in West Germany; indeed, throughout Western Europe. Parallel changes in Eastern Europe and in mainland China culminated in the virtual elimination of Soviet-style socialism by 1990.

Recession and Recovery

Jimmy Carter's policies produced a major recession. Ronald Reagan's produced a bigger one, the worst since the Great Depression, that dragged the rest of the world after us down into a slough. In the United States, this recession was followed by an economic recovery of unprecedented duration. The question, then, is, What caused the terrible recession and the long unbroken period of economic recovery?

The recession, it would appear, was brought about, first, by a deep, drastic cut in public spending on social programs. Social workers, civil servants, and government contractors were disemployed en masse. Out of work, they spent less. The poor and disadvantaged, deprived of welfare aid and support, spent less. Hence the slump of private consumption expenditures. Second, it was caused by the government's anti-inflation policy of forcing interest rates sky-high. As interest rates went up, the cost of investing in new or improved plant and equipment went up correspondingly. And spending on the renewal or expansion of plant and equipment, as well as in housing, declined precipitously. Inflation was ultimately checked not by high interest rates but in the old-fashioned way, through the impact of depression, mass unemployment, and the decline in consumer income. Nevertheless, even in the face of mass unemployment, excess industrial capacity, and wage concessions from weakened trade unions, prices in the corporate industrial sector, as in automobiles, never paused in their annual upward climb.

The subsequent recovery had a weak cause and a strong cause. Abandoning its "quantity of money" formula, the Federal Reserve Board reduced the rate of interest. While this produced no major upsurge of domestic investment to expand or to replace industrial capacity, at least it lowered the barriers to recovery. The central, overriding cause of recovery was the effect of an enormous infusion into the economy of new deficit-based spending. Never in America's history had government pumped in so much new spending, as indicated by the gap between what was taxed into and what was paid out from the government's coffers. The economy rode upward on the back of unprecedented deficits, hence of a vastly greater, cumulatively increasing national debt.[1]

The infusion of deficit-based spending took two forms: first, a reduction in taxes, with no commensurate decrease in public spending, that left more disposable income in consumers' pockets; second, a massive increase in military spending, not offset by an increase in taxation.

The initial reduction of public spending on social programs was accomplished quickly, and a drop in consumer spending and catastrophic recession followed at once. But time was required before enormous military appropriations could impact on the economy; time for planning, for the design and selection of weapons, for the taking of bids, for the negotiation of contracts, for the expansion of plants, for the design and installation of the equipment required in production, for the recruitment, training, and organization of scientists, engineers, and workers. It might take years until the budgeted increase in military spending would flow out as salaries and wages, as profits and dividends, and hence, as grist for the spending mill. Because the increased military spending was felt *later* than the reduced spending on social services, recovery followed the recession.

Thus, in true Keynesian fashion, deficit-based increments to the aggregate spending stream, whether manifest as public procurement or as more disposable income, cumulatively raised the level of aggregate spending, and sustained the process of economic recovery.

The Crisis Ahead

Throughout the 1980s, while their policies produced a stream of massive deficits and a cumulatively rising national debt, policymakers of every stripe outdid each other in their clamor for debt reduction, deficit reduction, and a balanced budget. The public has listened, and believed. With the onset of a new decade, the Warsaw Pact is gone. Now the Soviet Union has ceased to be a threat to the security of the United States or to its allies. Communism, longtime locus of capitalist paranoia, is dead. Suddenly, NATO is obsolete. Suddenly, the rationale that underlies our enormous military establishment, our subsidies to client states, and the expenditures that sustain the CIA has vanished. Suddenly, there is the undreamed-of opportunity for a balanced budget! Massive deficit and debt reduction is surely in the offing.

What sort of medicine is a balanced budget for an economy that has been sustained through a decade by, and whose recovery rests four-square upon, massive and continual infusions of new deficit-based spending? I venture that we are on the edge of a crisis; more, that it will be a very special crisis indeed, plagued not only by mass unemployment and inflation, but also by the collapse of, and the need to sustain and transform, the enormous industrial complex hitherto devoted to producing instruments of death.

Note

1. See Robert Eisner. *How Real is the Federal Deficit*. New York: Free Press, 1986.

2 • Questions

It was Keynesian policy for the public management of aggregate expenditure that presided over the golden decades of Western capitalism. Even when that policy was nominally abandoned, and political authority was exercised by its detractors, events confirmed the force of its argument. Deep recession followed upon the sudden cessation of public spending on social programs, and recovery rode the back of an enormous and continual infusion of deficit-based spending. Yet, before we comfortably return to Keynesian policy, there are questions that need to be answered.

There is stagflation. Have we any reason to suppose that the simultaneous and accelerating rise in both mass unemployment and inflation will not recur? Or if it does, that a Keynesian policy will not again be helpless before it? How can we comprehend this phenomenon, and resolve its evident contradiction to Keynesian theory?

There are monetary as well as fiscal technologies of control. What are their advantages and disadvantages, their weaknesses and strengths, in the management of aggregate expenditure?

There is deficit finance and the role it has played as the critical instrument of Keynesian expenditure management in maintaining American prosperity, and as its consequence, there is the accumulation of a national debt and the interest obligation it entails. What are the problems and costs of a national debt? How should these problems or costs be weighed in the balance for a policy choice?

Stagflation

Keynesian theory reflected a true observation of what occurred in the Great Depression. Industrial prices and wages were rigid. They resisted the pressure of a catastrophic drop in demand. Fixity was the fact. Keynesians did not look beyond the fact to its essential precondition. If they had, they would have encountered a fundamental contradiction. Neoclassical, microeconomics absolutely requires and operates on the assumption of free-moving, competitively determined price. The Keynesian macroanalytic absolutely requires and operates on the assumption of price fixity. Price is price. It cannot at once be fixed and free moving. How then, in spite of this fundamental contradiction, did microeconomics and macroeconomics coexist amicably for so long? Perhaps because the Keynesians made no incursions into the neoclassical territory to probe the behavior of the firm in order to explain why prices remained fixed when they did.

Price fixity during the depression decade must mean this at least; that industrial corporations and trade unions possessed and exercised so great a power over prices and wages that they could not be budged or shaken even by a cataclysmic drop in demand; not by armies of the unemployed, not by a vast excess of industrial capacity. Prices and wages could have remained unchanged only because that was within the power of the controlling corporations and trade unions, and because that expressed their policy. Prices and wages were not the reflex of any autonomous market-clearing mechanism. Prices and wages were a function of organizational policy. The relevant questions become, then: What are the determinants in formation of price and wage policies in the corporate industrial sector? What is the character of this policy-making choice?

This does not mean that the autonomous, market-clearing mechanism of neoclassical thought is wrong and should be discarded. It is false and misleading to suppose that any one big theory conveys the essence of the whole economy. Our economy breaks down into subeconomies, each operating under a particular set of rules, and each with problems and dangers particular to itself; among these, the neoclassical model has its place. Not all prices were unchanged during the depression decade. In the agricultural sector, prices plummeted. Our focus here, however, is on the subeconomy of massive industrial corporations with their unionized labor, embedded in a network of subcontracting and servicing satellites, dominating modern industry; the corporate industrial sector. It was in the corporate industrial sector that prices were fixed. It was in this sector that mass unemployment was generated. It is in this sector that prices and wages are a function of organizational policy, and it is here that the notion of an autonomous market-clearing mechanism should be discarded. We know little about how the entities of the corporate organizational sector formulate their policies, save, perhaps, that those policies represent the exercise of a power that is arbitrary in that it is neither determined by market forces, nor is it publicly accountable; that policies there are formulated under conditions of great uncertainty; that they are political, emerging through the interaction of numerous interests, and that convention, imitation, and role-playing in the matrix of an industrial community, and a sense of the boundaries of social acceptability, are of some explanatory significance.

The policies of corporations or of trade unions are not fixed in stone. Organizations are influenced by events. They can respond; they can learn. Their policies can and do change. It is easy to understand the fear that drove them to embrace a policy of holding fast, at all costs, to an existing order of wages and prices, given the utter desperation of the depression decade, when the economy seemed at the edge of a depth-less abyss. But in the 1950s and 1960s, with the state committed to offsetting any crisis in production and employment by an infusion of new spending, those fears diminished. Correspondingly, the character and rationale of wage/price policy in the corporate industrial sector changed. It came to express the general expectation of a steady rise in the standard of life. And as long as the demand for higher real incomes was matched by a compensating increase in productivity, those expectations could be satisfied without raising prices. Such was the sense of the ''wage price guidelines'' installed during the Kennedy administration, linking wage and price change to what had become an accustomed rate of productivity increase.

The rapid rise in productivity during the 1950s and 1960s satisfied built-in expectation of higher real incomes. Prices were remarkably stable. In the 1970s, that changed. The rate at which productivity was increasing declined sharply toward the null point. But the built-in expectations of higher real incomes continued apace. When there was no longer any compensating increase in productivity, the only way that labor or the firm might attempt to satisfy its income expectations was by forcing up prices. But any increase in real income realized as a consequence of that higher price policy would be eroded when other wage earners, firms, and industries followed suit with a consequent rise in the general price level, reducing the real value of the nominal rise in dollar incomes. The objective then became to beat the others to the inflationary punch, and to stay ahead of the pack in the race to inflate. With firms and industries pursuing that strategy, then, independently of change in aggregate demand or the level of unemployment, policy-based inflation must accelerate.

All this was gravely exacerbated in the late 1970s when OPEC reduced the world supply of petroleum, so that there was not merely a smaller increment of real income to be shared but a positive deprivation that had to be borne. The race to inflate accelerated as corporations and trade unions sought to escape the bite of deprivation. In government the primary objective of policy became to check rampant, policy-based inflation. For that, the accepted remedy was, in one way or another, to reduce aggregate demand.

Dominated by the need to control inflation, the government would no longer compensate for unemployment by infusing new spending into the expenditure stream. With aggregate spending held constant or declining, each successive policy-based rise in prices and wages must further increase the level of unemployment. Thus stagflation: an accelerating rise both of industrial prices and of industrial unemployment, simultaneously.

If one recognizes the organizational policy-making power behind the price rigidity that Keynes observed, the experience of stagflation is not a refutation but a logical evolution of Keynesian thought. With price a function of corporate industrial policy, mass unemployment will be the consequence either of prices held constant in the face of declining aggregate demand or of prices raised in the face of constant aggregate demand. The equation is exactly the same. Depression and stagflation are two sides of the same coin.

Even if we understand the character and cause of stagflation, and we can reconcile it to the rationale of Keynesian theory, we have yet to answer the question: Does the threat of stagflation limit or eliminate the possibility of a viable system for the management of public expenditure, or indeed of any system for achieving the twin goals of full employment and stable prices?

The Technologies of Control

To deal with inflation or mass unemployment, the state has relied on fiscal policy and or monetary policy: the former in the government's powers to create legal tender and to spend, to tax, and to borrow; the latter in the government's power to extend or contract the capacity of commercial banks to make credit available to individuals and corporations, thereby affecting the availability and price of loans to borrowers.

In considering these instruments of control, we recall some home truths.

1. Taxing, spending, borrowing can be carried on independently of each other. The government can spend without taxing or borrowing; it can tax without spending. In our terms, taxation reduces, and public spending adds to, the expenditure flow. By taxing and spending at once, the one offsetting the effect of the other, the government can remain neutral with respect to the level of aggregate expenditure.

2. When government spends without taxing, it does so by creating a new set of claims on the economy's fund of goods and services and on its capacity to produce goods and services. The claims may take the form of legal tender (money) or government bonds. In the first instance the claims are highly liquid and bear no interest. In the second instance they are less liquid but are interest-bearing.

3. Monetary policy is not an alternative to the public management of aggregate expenditure. It is another way of managing aggregate expenditure. Monetary policy can impact on the economy only and inasmuch as changes in the quantity of money held by commercial banks and the like produce change in the level of aggregate spending. Both the monetary and the fiscal technologies seek to control the management of aggregate spending. The question is: Which is the best able to do so? What are their comparative strengths and weaknesses? Should one or the other or some combination be preferred? How might they be developed to improve their efficiency and effectiveness? One must consider, first, their capacity for fast, firm, foresightful decision in the face of complex and swiftly changing circumstances, and second, with the decision taken and the objectives of policy given, their capacity to achieve those objectives by exercising an effective control over the magnitude and character of aggregate expenditure. For the ease and speed of decision-taking and the formulation of policy, the advantage in the United States lies with the monetary technology. Control is exercised by the autonomous Federal Reserve Board, where foresightful decisions by a body of experts under their chairman's command, based on carefully prepared information, can be swiftly taken, swiftly adapted, swiftly executed, swiftly changed. The locus of responsibility is clear. There is a minimum of extraneous intervention

or diversion. The freedom and decisiveness allowed to the Federal Reserve Board as a consequence of its autonomy also has its price. The board is not effectively answerable to the president, or to the Congress and the people. More than undemocratic, its decisions have the bias of experts caught in the inculcated confine of a narrow mode of thinking.

For the operation of the fiscal technology in the management of aggregate expenditure in the United States, there is now no locus of responsibility. The fiscal control of aggregate spending is submerged in the budgetary process, which operates through a complex of congressional and executive decisions that must take into account numerous and diverse responsibilities, obligations, and interests. Under present arrangements, it is probably impossible to have swift, foresighted, adaptable, decision taking and policy formation in the fiscal management of aggregate expenditure.

On the other hand, the fiscal technology has the greater capacity to control the magnitude and character of aggregate spending, and Keynesians have taken considerable strides in developing its innate potential for measured, precise, and flexible control. Through fiscal policy, spending can be immediately and directly pumped into or out from the expenditure stream. The character and distribution of aggregate spending can be reshaped, functionally, as between consumption and investment, demographically as between young and old, sick and well, rich and poor, and regionally as between government contractors in the East or in the West, or between those producing good X and those producing good Y. The monetary technology has no such potential. Its control of aggregate spending is loose and secondhand with consequences that are correspondingly unpredictable. It operates by indirection in attempting to affect the loan policies of commercial banks whose responses are as uncertain as that of those who might borrow from them.

There are also social costs and risks specific to each of the technologies of control. The monetary technology relies on the manipulation of interest rates. But interest rates impact also on income distribution and on economic growth. Whatever were their effects on inflation, the very high interest rates imposed by the Federal Reserve Board during the Carter and Reagan administrations, certainly blocked long-term domestic investment in research and development, in the installation of new machines and equipment, and in worker training for the purpose of raising productivity and increasing production, suffocating real growth and the possibility of a supply-side economics that might have drowned inflation with a surge of new, low-cost production. The influx of funds from abroad and the accumulation of a massive foreign debt, as another consequence of those very high domestic interest rates, will be explored later in our discussion in chapter 14 on the international flight of speculative cash balances.

The fiscal technology using deficit finance as its instrument in managing the level of aggregate spending generated a massive public debt with attendant costs and risks.

Deficit Finance and Non-Diversionary Expenditure

Here only that part of the public debt held by our own citizens and institutions (domestic debt) will be considered. Suppose that the objective of public policy is to combat a condition of mass unemployment, and for that purpose the political authority appropriates an additional $50 billion for medical spending by the sick and needy. Their increased expenditure will swell the incomes of the doctors, nurses, and hospitals who serviced them. These secondary beneficiaries will respend a part of their additional income. Those who gain from their respending will in turn respend a part of what they have received. And so forth. By the time the impact has exhausted itself, the level of aggregate expenditure will have been increased by some multiple of the original appropriation, say threefold, to a total increase in aggregate expenditure of $150 billion.

If the Congress had raised the funds through taxation, it would simply have diverted spending from the private to the public sector, taking out of the spending stream as much as it had put in, with the contraction on the one side offsetting the expansion on the other, and nothing added to the level of aggregate spending. Where its purpose is to raise the level of aggregate demand, government spending must not be a diversion of private spending but a net addition to the spending flow. So, instead of diverting expenditure through taxation, the government borrows the funds. The borrowing-spending transaction is considered to be substantially non-diversionary. In borrowing, it is supposed, the government does not take as much out of the spending stream as it puts back in with an equivalent public expenditure. Such is the rationale of public borrowing, when the objective of government is to raise the level of aggregate spending.

Problems of the Public Debt?

The 1980s witnessed an enormous increase in the size of the American public debt, and because of the rise in interest rates, a much larger increase in the size of its interest obligations. Concern for the public debt looms large on the political horizon. What then are the detriments of the public debt? Why indeed should public debt be considered a problem?

Certain allegations concerning the problems of the debt cannot be accepted a priori.

1. It is alleged that future generations will be obliged to pay for the profligacy of the generation that did the borrowing; that in incurring a national debt, we are imposing on future generations a positive deprivation. In the first instance, consider only the domestic debt.

Suppose those future generations are obliged to repay the national debt incurred in our time. To whom would they repay it? It would be repaid to those selfsame future generations. And since any generation that chooses to makes repayments on the national debt would make those repayments to itself, it is hard to imagine how a nation as a whole could be deprived, let alone bankrupted, by shifting income from one set of its pockets to another set. The existence of a large debt may make things politically difficult for future generations, but it will deprive them of none of their resources. Therefore, it cannot reduce their real, full-employment GNP, or necessitate a lowering in their per cap-ita income and standard of life.

It would seem true, however, that the repayment of foreign debt, or the payment of interest on a foreign debt incurred by us, would impose a real burden on future generations, depriving them of some of their resources and their economic product. A foreign debt, moreover, which can be withdrawn with any shift in the financial wind, may introduce a dangerously unstable element into the system.

2. It is alleged that the marketing of new government bonds competes with the marketing of new corporate securities for a share of the limited funds available for investment, so that if more is allotted to the purchase of government securities, less will be left for the procurement of corporate securities; hence, adding to the national debt through the sale of government securities crowds out private investment. This argument overlooks a key relationship. When the government borrows and spends, just as when it taxes and spends, the funds it collects may

move from one set of banks to another, but they do not leave the banking system. Neither the magnitude of cash balances nor the ratio of cash to deposits is changed; nor, therefore, is the capacity of the banking system to make new loans and to expand the base for private investment affected.

3. It has been alleged that a rising national debt shakes Wall Street's confidence in the American future, threatening a stock market collapse. Pundits blamed "black Monday" and the 1987 stock market crash on the size of the national debt, and warned that only through a return to a balanced budget could stocks resume their upward climb. In fact, the stock market had risen to unprecedented heights as a corollary to an unprecedented rate of increase in the size of the American public debt, and subsequently continued on its upward climb while the national debt continued to increase.

Other detriments, which all have to do with the obligation to pay interest on the public debt, are hard to deny. The horrendous increase in that obligation was a direct function of governmental policy, having as much to do with the high interest rates imposed on both private and public borrowing by the anti-inflationary monetary policies of the Federal Reserve Board as it had with any increase in the magnitude of the debt itself. As a consequence of that increase in debt obligations, we currently have a situation where real wages are decreasing, profits are low, and the increment of economic growth accrues as never before in interest payments.

1. If there is a psychological limit on the level of permissible taxation, the burden of taxation required to pay interest on the debt can crowd out tax-financed public expenditures of positive worth to society.

2. The payment of interest on the public debt constitutes a transfer of income from the poorer (taxpayers) to the richer (bondholders), so that the distribution of income in the United States, already the most unequal in the industrialized world, becomes more unequal still.

3. Wages, salaries, and profits are taxed in order to pay interest on the public debt. In that way, those forms of income payments that do provide a positive incentive to work and to invest are transformed into an income payment without incentive value. Interest payments are not only without incentive value, they provide a cushion against the pressures to work or to undertake the risks of business ventures. Correspondingly, the source of economic dynamism is diminished.

3 • Answers

We have asked some challenging questions. Now we will tentatively propose some answers. In so doing, we will stake out a path toward a viable policy for full employment and price stability. We do not propose to abandon or replace the public management of aggregate spending. The public management of aggregate spending has, we believe, already established its worth. We would improve it: first, and least controversially, in the reform of the technologies of decision making and control; second, with regard to deficit finance and the public debt; and finally, in dealing with stagflation.

We will propose policy changes and a reform of the instruments of policy implementation. The proposals made envisage not a larger or more expensive apparatus of governance, but a stronger, more positive state, with more encompassing responsibilities and powers. Some will consider a stronger, more responsible state as itself a problem and a danger. We see it, rather, as an opportunity and a necessity in our time.

The advent of a policy to maintain full employment and price stability through the management of aggregate spending was a revolutionary step in the development of an economic role for the American state. The policy was new, but there was nothing new in the technologies employed for its implementation. It operated through techniques devised during generations past for other purposes entirely. The technology of expenditure management needs an overhaul.

Rationalizing the Instrument of Control

We speak of expenditure management, but who in the American system is the manager? There is, in fact, no one in charge, no locus of control, no point of answerability. Responsibilities are scattered among the bureaucracies and fatally split between the Treasury and the Federal Reserve Board. Prerequisite to a rational and democratic management is a clear locus of control, vested with the powers, bearing the responsibility, and answerable for performance to Congress and to the electorate.

Selective Controls

Policy has been limited to the control of the gross magnitude of aggregate expenditure. Given the probable nature of the oncoming crisis, where the state must confront not only the general problem of mass unemployment, but the structural collapse of the defense-oriented sector of industry as well, there is the need for selective controls and the capacity for, and a strategy to affect, patterns of spending. The agency charged with expenditure management, for example, should be able to require variation in the terms at which different forms of credit are made available, in order, say, to inhibit consumer credit and consumption expenditure while encouraging spending on real investment; or to discourage investment that does not add to the production potential, for example, in the purchase of land and of old securities, or in corporate takeovers and the forcing of mergers, or in the shifting of manufacturing operations to where labor is unorganized and cheap; while encouraging investment, such as in research and development or in the replacement or extension of industrial plant and equipment, that can reasonably be equated to higher productivity and/or to an increase in production.

Patterns of expenditure could also be influenced to ensure balance in economic growth or in the recovery from recession by directing public procurement so as to favor regions and industries where deep pools of unemployment persist while labor bottlenecks and inflationary pressures prevail elsewhere.

There is nothing intrinsically new about selective controls on expenditures. Fiscal and monetary practice are replete with devices for selective control. Financial operations have been established to make cheaper credit available for particular purposes and/or to a particular clientele, for example, students, farmers, exporters, veterans, and homeowners. The character of commercial bank loans is variously controlled. The use of credit for the purchase of securities on margin is controlled. There have been tax allowances, exemptions, subsidies conferring inducements, and benefits on favored activities. What is lacking, and what is needed, is the systematic and flexible use of such tools and devices in a purposeful strategy of expenditure management, where the primary objective is full employment and price stability.

Prespecification of Programs and the Need for Speed

Suppose an agency is in charge, answerable to Congress and responsible for managing the level of aggregate spending, using both fiscal and monetary instruments in the design and implementation of its strategy. If that agency foresees a recession, or if there is a sudden unforeseen downturn in the economy, then half the battle is to respond quickly with remedial measures. Neither a foresighted nor a quick fiscal response is possible, given the present organization and practices of American government. The request by the agency charged with the management of aggregate spending for a tax reduction or a tax increase, or for an increase or decrease in the level of public spending, must wait its turn in the passage of a multitude of requests through the executive, and then the congressional, budgeting mill, where interests and considerations unrelated to the most urgent need to forestall an impending recession will have priority.

To overcome this problem, and to enable a quick response to the exigencies of the economy, Congress should prespecify a schedule of approved programs considered desirable but dispensable, and hence, appropriate when the task is to turn on or turn off the expenditure spigot for project spending and/or tax reductions or tax surcharges. These programs would be diverse in their regional and industrial focus, so that they could be vectored to the specifics of regional and industrial need. The agency charged with expenditure management, choosing from among them, would be able immediately to activate a set of its choice, and would be required to deactivate its chosen set depending on economic conditions, as measured by indicators specified by Congress; for example, programs might be activated when unemployment reaches an indicated level, and deactivated when the rate of inflation reaches an indicated level.

Forward Planning

The objective of expenditure management is not only to respond to the pressure of immediate events, but also to offset the threat of future crisis. In order to anticipate such a threat, American economists have developed complex forecasting models of the economy. To the same end, an innovative technique, indicative planning, was developed in France, based on the knowledge that large industrial entities, which in France are both private and public, plan their real investment expenditures years in advance. At five-year intervals, the French Indicative Planning Authority, which was the agency responsible for the management of aggregate expenditure in France, required all these industrial entities, both public and private, to reveal to it the magnitude and character of their real investment plans for the next five years, and, periodically, to report any changes in those plans. Thus, the Planning Authority had more than an academic forecast with which to work. It had a positive statement of business plans and commitments. If the total of those planned investment expenditures by private corporations and public agencies was less than or in excess of the desired level of aggregate expenditure, the Planning Authority would act through direct consultation with and pressure on the private and public industrial entities to modify their investment plans, or on government agencies to adapt their fiscal or monetary policies to eliminate the stimulus to inflation or recession.

The United States, for the sake of a more foresighted management of our aggregate spending, should follow this French example. Administrative underpinnings to undertake the task of indicative planning will be proposed in part 2.

The Practice of Expenditure Management

In the decades before stagflation unsaddled Keynesian policy, the actual practice of expenditure management in the United States was only occasional and very crude, amounting to nothing more than willingness to incur deficits in response to the hard blows of recession. The aforementioned reforms would, for the first time, enable a control that is efficient, foresighted, flexible, selective, and responsible to the Congress, the executive, and the people.

Is a Steady Infusion
of Non-Diversionary Spending Needed?

At the heart of the Keynesian program is the conscious and deliberate use of deficit finance as the means of adding to aggregate expenditure *without diverting* spending from the private sector or from other public programs; hence, enabling a controlled quantum of non-diversionary spending. Deficit finance–based public expenditure is considered a system for the non-diversionary infusion of new spending.

Is the infusion of non-diversionary spending inflationary? If it pushes up the price level, it is. If it does not, it is not. What is germane is not the infusion of non-diversionary spending, but the effects of a change in the level of aggregate spending, whatever the means by which it has been brought about. It was the Keynesian contention that for the corporate industrial sector, where prices are rigid, and when unemployment is rife, the consequence of an increase in aggregate demand would be to reemploy workers, and to increase production until the work force is fully employed, or plants are operating at full capacity. Then, if aggregate demand keeps rising, the price level would be forced to climb as well.

Republicans are proud, as well they may be, of the long-sustained economic recovery following the great recession of the 1980s, reducing the number of unemployed and creating job opportunities for labor newcomers, all at an acceptable level of inflation. The corollary and, presumably, the cause of that long-sustained recovery was an unprecedentedly large annual infusion (neither deliberated nor intended) of non-diversionary spending, putting deficit-based dollars into the pockets of consumers through tax concessions, or into the hands of military contractors through defense expenditures. This experience suggests the likelihood that our present economy requires a continuous but controlled infusion of non-diversionary expenditure as a prerequisite to sustained prosperity; that a gap is continuously appearing between the optimal and the spontaneously produced levels of aggregate spending, needing continuously to be filled; that the need for a steady infusion of non-diversionary spending is not unusual or deviant, but is normal for our time.

There is nothing calamitous about the prospect of maintaining an annual infusion of new spending. On the contrary, it offers the opportunity of achieving, without pain, some of our neglected social goals. The calamity is in the accumulative growth of the public debt and the interest obligation it entails, which is the consequence, not of nondiversionary spending per se, but of the use of deficit finance as the technique of infusion. But must deficit finance be used as the means of maintaining the required level of non-diversionary expenditure?

Deficit Finance as an Instrument of Expenditure Management

In order to increase private plus public spending, government borrows and accumulates a public debt. Surely, there is something suspect in that. Government borrowing was developed as a means of reducing spending in the private sector. Borrowing is a contract wherein the borrower pays the lender a fixed sum (interest) and in return, the lender surrenders his right to spend the amount of the loan (the principal) for an agreed period of time.

Through such contractual arrangements, public borrowing was traditionally used as a means of reducing private spending by immobilizing the spending potential of those from whom the government borrowed. In time of war, for example, when the objective is to minimize private demand so that resources might be shifted away from production for the civilian consumer to satisfy an omnivorous military need, borrowing is intended to reduce spending in the private sector by "mopping up" what cannot be gotten at through taxation. Yet here, deficit finance which, like taxation, was devised in order to reduce spending, is being used as a means of increasing it.

Admitting this, Keynesians might defend the use of deficit finance as an instrument of non-diversionary spending on the following grounds.

1. The lender, holding government bonds as an easily convertible, interest-bearing asset in lieu of cash, knows himself to be as rich as he was before. Therefore, the lender will not be motivated to save more, that is, to spend less (as he presumably would in order to replace a part of his wealth that was taxed away). Hence, the increase of spending on the public side via the sale of bonds would be only partially offset by a decrease of spending caused by borrowing in the private sector.

2. A period of recession, when the state would want to increase

the level of aggregate spending, is precisely the time when investment opportunities in the private sector are likely to be few and far between, with the financial system well below its lending potential. Hence, banks or other financial institutions or rich individuals will purchase government bonds with funds that would not have been spent on consumption or for real investment, but would have lain idle.

Expenditure Management
without a Public Debt

The best that can be said for the use of deficit finance as an instrument of non-diversionary spending is that borrowing does not reduce aggregate spending by as much as taxation would. When the government borrows, and spends what it borrows, more is put into than is taken out of the flow of aggregate spending. It is evident, nevertheless, that deficit finance used as a technique to raise the level of aggregate spending is inefficient, because it must divert some private spending, and costly, because of the aforementioned burdens of a public debt that it imposes. We ask, then, whether deficit finance is the only feasible way to increase systematically the magnitude of aggregate spending. Can we devise a more efficient system of non-diversionary spending— one that does not impose on society the burdens of public debt?

Our answer is clear and simple. Certainly we can. But given the strength of the mythos of inflation, the public's mind must be prepared for it. And legislators must understand it as a delicate instrument to be used only when it is the objective of policy to raise the level of total spending.

Consider the traditional neoclassical image of the economy, where autonomous price moves freely to equate supply and demand. With supply conditions given, the price level must be a function of aggregate demand. If aggregate demand (or total spending) goes down, so does the price level, hence deflation. If aggregate demand goes up, so does the price level, hence inflation.

Under these conditions, for an economy operating in the mode of the neoclassical model, an increase in aggregate demand (i.e., an addition to total spending) must force the price level higher. Alternatively, in the conditions of the modern corporate industrial economy, an increase in aggregate demand may, instead, raise the level of production and employment. Either way, the higher prices or the increase in employment and production will be brought about by an increase in aggregate spending. The effect will be the same, whatever brought that increase in aggregate spending about: whether it was the consequence of the changed expectations and free decisions of individuals to save less (hence, to consume more); or the stimulus to business spending of new investment opportunities; or if it was induced by lower interest rates under the aegis of the Federal Reserve Board; or if it was the government's choice to spend more undiverted dollars to purchase goods and services, or to lower taxes without a compensatory reduction of the level of public spending, leaving more dollars in the pockets of consumers. As long as the net increase in aggregate spending is the same, the effect on employment and production or on the price level will be the same. One source of incremental spending, can be no more inflationary than any other.

It will not matter, as far as the impact on prices or production is concerned, whether the non-diversionary dollars that are used for government procurement or that are put into the pockets of consumers are borrowed or freshly printed. A given increase in aggregate demand may or may not be desirable, but it will be no more and no less inflationary, whether it is based on an influx of borrowed dollars or printed dollars.

The Interest-free Public Debt

Suppose, under the instruction of Congress, the Federal Reserve Board, as our central bank, opened an account for the U.S. Treasury, authorizing the Treasury to spend from that account to some prespecified limit, and the Treasury did so. The government would nominally have incurred a debt to the Federal Reserve Board, itself an agency of that government. Interest would not be paid on that "debt." The 27 percent of the national debt now owned by the Federal Reserve Board and by other agencies of the American government is, in effect, interest-free. The existence of this massive interest-free debt should be seen in relation to the strategy of expenditure management.

Public spending financed through an interest-free line of credit established by the central bank would constitute a convenient system of non-diversionary public spending. Thus, for example, at the behest of Congress, the Federal Reserve Board would open an account in the name of the United States Secretary of the Treasury for an amount specified by the Congress, from which he could withdraw cash or against which he could write checks at his discretion for the purpose of authorized public expenditures. Such spending would constitute a debt on the books of the Federal Reserve Board, but a debt that would impose no obligation to pay interest. This system would serve as a bookkeeping device. Since it would operate through an established and respected agency, it could serve to shield non-diversionary public spending against the public's irrational fears of "printing press money." But in truth the system would be financing public expenditure through the authorized expenditure of "printing press money." Just as now, when the Federal Reserve Board that charges no interest on the government securities in its possession, purchases such securities as an incident of monetary policy, and finances the transaction with new, freshly printed federal reserve notes.

In the condition of economic depression, when a skilled and ready labor force is without work, the apparatus of production is idle, and the objective of public policy is to add to, that is, to inflate, the magnitude of aggregate spending, the question ought to be: What is the most effective, least costly way of inflating the level of aggregate spending? It certainly matters whether that increase is on target. It matters whether the response of industry to an increase in aggregate spending is to raise its prices rather than to increase production. What does not matter is whether the new spending is done with old money or with new, freshly printed bills, with a check drawn on a private account at a commercial bank, or with a check drawn on a public account at the central bank.

Problems and Dangers
of an Interest-free National Debt

We recommend the creation of interest-free debt by the central bank under the control of the agency charged with the management of aggregate demand as an efficient system for funding non-diversionary spending, without the burden of an interest-bearing public debt. This would as well enable the controlled, painless repayment of the existing interest-bearing public debt. But in eliminating the heavy burden of interest and repayment obligations, it would introduce other sorts of problems, certainly of a lesser order, but problems and dangers nevertheless.

Whether to finance its transactions it prints new money or sells its securities (borrows), the government invests the economy with an additional set of paper assets: securities in the one instance, cash in the other. In either case, the wealth in private possession, that is, the magnitude of the privately held claims on goods and services that have been or could be produced, is increased. The difference between an increase in the quantity of cash and an increase in the quantity of public securities is that, of the two sorts of asset, cash is the more mobile, entails no obligation on the part of government to pay interest, and in the American banking system as it is presently constituted, gives more leeway to commercial banks to expand their lending. A system of expenditure management that would increase aggregate spending through the institutionalized use of an interest-free debt must also be sensitive to the volatility of cash, and be enabled to tax cash out of the economy with the same facility that it pumped cash into the economy, and it must be in a position to constrain, as needed, the lending potential of commercial banks.

The funding of non-diversionary spending by allowing drawing rights to the Treasury (or to whatever agency charged with the management of aggregate expenditure) on an account opened at the central bank, with corresponding measures to control the volatility of cash in the banking system, would enable, for the first time, a rational fiscal instrument tailored to the task of managing aggregate spending, avoiding the costly and functionless burden of an increase in the interest-bearing public debt.

Confronting Stagflation

It was the experience of stagflation, and of the rise of prices and unemployment, simultaneously, that destroyed the American commitment, under Keynesian aegis, to manage aggregate spending. Nor is there any reason to suppose that the race to inflate, where increasing unemployment is a function of rising prices, will not recur. It hangs like a pall over the possibility of any policy for full employment and stable pricing.

The root cause of stagflation is the power of corporations and trade unions to set prices and wages as a matter of organizational policy. In fact, there can be no security from stagflation, no possible assurance of price stability or full employment, unless that policy-making power in the corporate organizational sector is destroyed or controlled. To destroy it would require an unthinkable degree of industrial fragmentation. The only other option is some form of price/wage control, coupled with the management of aggregate spending.

This is not a novel notion. From Franklin Roosevelt to Richard Nixon, every president faced with inflation stood ready to exercise some form of influence or control on price/wage policy in the corporate industrial sector: selective, informal pressures denigrated as "jawboning," quasi enforcement under published wage/price guidelines, or the imposition of a wage/price freeze under Richard Nixon. Rough and ready as they were, these measures served to maintain a high degree of price stability throughout earlier postwar decades; until the laissez-faire policies of President Carter; although one recalls that Carter had his "Chief Inflation Fighter" (one chief, no Indians), who did a sort of ritual dance on television after each new wave of price and wage increases. Under President Reagan there was not even a pretense of direct influence or control.

We do not envisage a universal system of price/wage control, but one applied only to prices and wages in the corporate-industrial sector. In that sector there is no question of introducing price/wage controls since, via the formation of organizational policies, prices and wages are already controlled. The issue rather is who will participate and what will be taken into account in the formation of wage and price policy in that sector. We propose systematic participation by a public agency in the formation of such policy when and if there is a repeat encounter with the phenomenon of stagflation.

The character of the agency and the system of control that is chosen would be, of course, of great importance. In part 2 we look to the experience of Japan's famous Ministry of International Trade and Industry to better understand the nature and competence of a public agency that might effectively participate in the formation of corporate industrial policies.

The Problem of Distributional Justice

The successful operation of a system of wage/price control shifts the determination of who gets what from the random forces of the market to the political arena and the realm of public choice, where the issue of, and the demand for, distributional justice is bound to arise. We have, alas, no accepted criterion of distributional justice, and the possibility of ever developing one is, to say the least, uncertain. Indeed, the possibility of avoiding future hatred and strife over income shares depends on our response to another set of questions: Can we accelerate the advance of technology? The rise in productivity? The rate of growth? For it is infinitely easier to devise an acceptable distribution of additions to a rising level of wealth than it is to distribute a fixed or shrinking net product, where the rise of one must drag another down, where any increase for one can only be at the expense of another.

PART 2

THE QUESTION OF POLITICAL COMPETENCE: MITI AND AIM

Memorandum

To: Reader
From: Author
Subject: Can the American government develop the competence the proposed economic reforms will require?

1. The policies and reforms proposed in this book will require a positive state able to (1) participate in the formation of corporate industrial policies, (2) participate in certain facets of industrial management, and (3) spearhead and coordinate targeted industrial development. At present, no public agency in the United States is equipped for these tasks.

2. Can an agency able to undertake these tasks be developed in the American political system? To answer that question Japan's famous Ministry of International Trade and Industry (MITI), key agency of the positive Japanese state, is examined and analyzed in some depth, taking into account its history, powers, responsibilities, experience and contributions, system of recruitment and training, and the political and economic context of its operations.

3. Chapter 5 proposes the formation of the Agency for Industrial Management (AIM) to undertake MITI's functions in the American economic and political context, specifying the nature of its tasks and the problems of its formation.

4 • MITI and the Instrumentality of Economic Reform

Japan's Advantage

The day is gone when the American could think he had everything to teach and nothing to learn from others. The battered American industrialist wants to know, and a host of scholars, journalists, and specialists aggressively seek to discover, to propagate, and to publish, the secrets of Japanese success. In this regard, their attention is concentrated primarily on management practice in the industrial corporation, with ample attention given to the cultural factor and the general operation of the economy.[1] But the Japanese industrial corporation and its operation is part of an integral system, and at the heart of that system is the Japanese state. Among the Americans who study, write about, and consider themselves experts on Japan, there is, as the consequence of our ideological bias, a curious reluctance to recognize the positive and powerful role of the Japanese state in the organization of technological progress and industrial advance. The exception is Chalmer Johnson, on whose work I will largely rely.[2] Indeed, what differentiates the amazing achievements of the Japanese economy in the decades after the end of the American occupation, as compared to an earlier, far less impressive performance, is the preeminent role during the latter years of the Japanese Ministry of International Trade and Industry. In this chapter, we ask what can be learned from the development and operation of MITI that is relevant to an understanding, not only of what the state should do, but also of what the state should be, in regard not only to its policies, but also to the instrumentality for their formulation and implementation.

43

By the passage of its history, Japan has a particular and critical cultural advantage. During the European Renaissance, there emerged the self-sufficing, self-deciding figure of autonomous man. In the centuries that followed, Western society and civilization was shaped to reflect and accommodate his values and needs. The sovereign individual became free to act as he willed, and consume as he would, within a political and economic space delineated by political rights and the prerogatives of property, and to engage in discourse, social intercourse, and trade with others so disposed. The experience of autonomous man and his world has shaped our values, is codified in our laws, is propagated as ideological liberalism, and is "scientifically expressed" in neoclassical economic theory.

Although the images remain, the reality of this world of man has largely gone. We are, all of us, caught in a transition of western civilization. Once we dwelled, and our minds were shaped, in that world of man. Now we are leaving or have left that world for a universe of systems. The autonomy of the individual has been displaced. We live, instead, under conditions of extreme interdependence. We operate no longer in sovereign spaces of a social grid. Instead, each one of us occupies a niche in a system; a niche that determines our role, our rights, our prerogatives, our outlets for effective choice and action; in fact, we occupy a number of niches in a complex of systems whose operations are beyond our ken or control. If we participate in control, it is through the politics of organization.

Although we live in the universe of systems, our thought still dwells with the images of man in the world of man. Our perceptions have not kept pace with our experience. Thus, the prevailing representation of the economy was formed and frozen as neoclassical theory two centuries ago, though encountered realities have greatly changed since then. Ideological lag is a problem behind our problems.

Japan carries the burdens of a different history, but in one respect, Japan has the advantage over all the rest of us. Compared to every other advanced industrial society, only Japan entered the modern universe of systems without ever going through the phase of individualized choice in the world of man. Only Japan has not had to overcome the hang-ups of ideological liberalism in adapting to the realities of our industrialized world.

Japan never left the universe of systems. Before, her systems were feudal, closed. Central emphasis was on their refinement and perfection, and the perpetuation of the traditional. Now, her systems are open and dynamic, with central emphasis on transformation and growth. But in both feudal and modern organizations, Japanese life was lived in niches that determined role and function, rights and obligations, and the relationship of the one to the whole. The ingrained and unshaken capacities to comprehend the character and prerequisites of organization, to think clearly and creatively about organizations, to act collectively and to interact effectively within and as part of organizations, is the enduring cultural advantage of the Japanese. Given this cultural advantage, Japan has developed instruments of collective action that have proven extraordinarily effective in our time.[3]

This book is concerned with goals and problems of the United States, and to some degree of other countries, into the twenty-first century. We propose an agenda, questions and answers, problems and solutions, for the postmodern state. But no agenda, no solution to the problems that confront us, can transcend our capacity for governance or go beyond the reach of our instrumentalities of positive public action. For the solution of its most critical problems, as we just demonstrated in the instance of full employment and price stability, the United States certainly will require a greater capacity for governance and the development of new instruments for positive public action. We focus in this chapter on an agency of the Japanese state that has been its key instrument in shaping and developing the Japanese economy, for we believe there are lessons to be learned in examining this facet of Japanese experience.

Operation MITI

Education, Recruitment, and Training

We propose to describe the history of MITI and its operation from the ground up, and later, to consider what can be learned thereby. We consider first the recruitment and training of MITI's operating personnel.[4]

The Japanese educational system selects the highest talent for the public service. In its preuniversity phase, Japanese education is excruciatingly demanding, difficult, and selective. It competitively divides its student body into successively narrower echelons in a hierarchy of tested abilities. At the educational apex are the universities. The peak among them is the Tokyo Imperial University, and within that university, as the elite of elites, is the Tokyo School of Law, where in spite of the name, training is not legalistic, but geared to the public service.

Each year, some fifty thousand top university graduates sit for the Higher-Level Public Officials Examination. Of these, perhaps one thousand pass, the bulk of whom are from the Tokyo Imperial University, most from the School of Law. The ministries then recruit from among the eligible. Approximately the top quarter of the law school graduates enter the government service. The rest go to prefectural governments, public corporations, banks, and business companies of all kinds, destined to the role of an elite leadership.

An annual cohort of fifteen to twenty-five are recruited to join the five hundred or so higher-level officials at MITI. Lower-level officials also are recruited through competitive examinations to work as specialists. The agency, with a total employment of about three thousand, is by American standards, very small and tight, attracting to itself the most talented of oncoming generations. With recruitment, the training begins.

Each new recruit of the class of, say, 1988, will form a relation of junior to senior with one of the cohort of 1987. Thenceforth, the senior will play the role of patron, supporter, guide, and teacher to his junior. That senior is himself a junior in relation to his guide and patron in the class of 1986, and so forth. These vertical relations remain throughout the officials' careers.

Each recruit will be sent "around the track," from task to task, abroad and in Japan, in bureau after bureau, so that he might comprehend and acquire the capacity to handle all the functions of the agency, and create and cement relations with others at the same level within the agency, or with those outside, with whom the agency must deal. Under the observation of its seniors, the cohort demonstrates its talents and capacities.

Promotion and Retirement

Each member of an incoming cohort will be promoted by seniority until, after fifteen to twenty years of service, he has attained the rank of section chief. Beyond that, since there are not enough higher positions to go around, the cohort will be thinned out, its members selectively retired.

The vice-minister, who heads the agency, as a matter of established practice names his own successor. When the new head of the agency is chosen, all the members of his cohort, or earlier cohorts, resign or are retired so that no one in the agency will be the new agency head's senior. The agency does not abandon its retirees who, as they say, in retiring, "descend from heaven." Nor do those who retire sever their link to the agency. As the superbly trained elite of elites, conditioned to tasks of great responsibility at the nexus of politics and industry, they move with ease into leading positions in politics (the Japanese Diet is dominated by former officials of the ministries), private enterprise, or public corporations, banks, or universities, thus deepening, solidifying, and extending the network of linkages to the agency center.

Formation and Implementation of Policy

Although the agency's organization is based on seniority and hierarchy, the new cohorts are given an extraordinary role in the formation of MITI policy. To capitalize on their fresh vision, MITI has "a unique institution known as the Laws and Ordinances Examination Committee," with its membership from the lowly assistant section chief level. There, "all major policies of the ministry are introduced and no new policy can be initiated without its approval."[5] Not only does this open a space for the "new vision" of youth, but the goals that are introduced by that committee at that level, become the personal commitment of those who will be with the agency over the years required for their achievement.

MITI's powers are very broad, but are of the nature of leverage, pressure, and influence rather than of command. Possessing its own sources of revenue, it is financially independent of the Ministry of Finance as well as of the national budget. Its officials are indoctrinated in a samurai-like code of service marked by discipline, austerity, an unlimited work commitment, pride and self-belief, and the sense that they bear the responsibility for Japan's future.

Who else participates in the formulation of Japan's highest economic policy? While ideas and influences may variously infiltrate, the only opportunity for the systematic participation of others is through "deliberation councils," where business leaders and academics are invited to discuss problems of the economy with MITI officials. What, then, is the role of those elected to the Japanese Diet, the prime minister and his cabinet; that is, of the Japanese government in the formulation of the highest economic policy?

In the relationship of officialdom to government, the great distinction between authority and control in Japan is made explicit. Once, the emperor, "Son of Heaven," reigned, but the shogunate ruled. Now, the Diet reigns, but the ministries rule. Authority resides in the Diet, but control is firmly exercised by the ministry bureaucrats. The Diet is not truly a deliberative body: it has no independent staff. In the normal course of events, all important legislation originates in, is formulated by, and is executed through the ministries, including taxation, tariffs, and financial appropriations.

The Diet wields the rubber stamp. It legitimizes the work of the bureaucracies, and shields them from external pressures. But the Diet, in its composition and character, also reflects the balance of interests and the coalition of forces that currently form the working basis of the sociopolitical system. The bureaucracies accept and accommodate that balance of interests and coalition of forces. In rare but sometimes critical instances, when built-in bureaucratic imperatives conflict with the changing needs and values of society at large, as in the 1960s when a halt to the painful spread of pollution conflicted with the bureaucratic goal of rapid economic growth, the Diet can, and has, initiated new policy and the transformation of bureaucratic goals.

A Society of Autonomous Groups

Japan crossed the threshold of modernity directly from millennia of feudalism, and modern Japan, like feudal Japan, is a society of tightly bound, autonomous, self-perpetuating groups that, like MITI and the industrial corporations, are at once social communities and functional organizations. Within the group, as part of the group, the individual finds identity, and his position in the group determines his responsibilities and defines his prerogatives. Groups are intensely competitive in the struggle for place and power, with some rising into, and others descending from, positions of dominance.

Each of the ministries is such a group, striving for self-perpetuation and dominance. The ministries, as a whole, constitute a cluster of autonomous groups, held together by shared tasks and responsibilities, and torn apart by jurisdictional rivalries and policy conflicts.[6]

So, also, there are clusters of autonomous industrial groups called *zaibatsu;* sets of companies and their satellites, each including a trading company and a more or less complete set of those industries that have been targeted by MITI for development, organized as a rounded industrial community. Before World War II, each industrial grouping was bound together by family ownership. Today, their strongest internal tie is a kind of mother bank at the center.

Over time, power and preeminence has shifted. It continues to shift between the different *zaibatsu* and between MITI and the *zaibatsu.*

Origins

The Meiji restoration initially sought to modernize Japan with industries created and controlled by government. In 1880, its policy changed. It undertook the promotion of private capitalism. It sold its industrial properties, and offered support and subsidy to private enterprise.[7] The immediate beneficiaries were the big trading companies that bought, and with government support, developed the new industries.

In 1881, the Ministry of Agriculture and Commerce (MAC) was established. Although it built and operated the Yawata Steel Company, its primary concern was with agriculture. At the time, Japan's economy was primarily agricultural, and even its major export industry, silk textiles, was an agricultural offshoot. In 1925, the Ministry of Agriculture and Commerce became the Ministry of Agriculture and Forestry. Its commerce side became the Ministry of Commerce and Industry (MCI). The Tokyo Law School graduates who entered MCI at that time were of the first cohort to be recruited into the ministries through competitive examination. That same cohort, after a long apprenticeship, would control MITI, and through MITI, the post–World War II economy of Japan.

In 1927, MCI convened a deliberation council, which included Japan's leading businessmen and academics, to chart its tasks and priorities. There emerged a policy of Western-style "rationalization," with emphasis on "scientific management," the public provision of information as the basis of business choice, the subsidized production of import substitutes, and cartelization or "self-rule" among the *zaibatsu.*

Depression and War

In 1930, the Great Depression struck Japan. As elsewhere, in Japan the first response was fiscal austerity and deflation, which, as it did elsewhere, augmented the disaster. The year 1931 opened three distinct and decisive paths of policy development.

The Ministry of Finance, under Takakashi Korekiyo, pumped a stream of incremental (deficit-based) spending into the sagging economy. That policy can be credited with Japan's extraordinary performance during the depression decade. From 1931 to 1939, production more than doubled.

In 1931, MCI launched its two-pronged Yoshino-Kishi line, promoting heavy industry, and installing an "industrial self-control" that gave the rules laid down by the *zaibatsu* the force of law. As a consequence, to MCI's later consternation, the decisive economic power shifted into the hands of the great industrial families, and would remain there until the end of World War II.

That same year, Japan invaded Manchuria. The military, as another autonomous group within Japanese society, began its bid for supreme power, terrorizing all opposition through a series of political assassinations. In 1937, the pace of foreign conquest accelerated. A full-scale war against China was coupled with the development of a framework for the total mobilization of industry in preparation for a wider conflict. MCI officials were the workhorses of the regime. Seconded to Manchuria, they initiated, planned, and managed the building and operation of a new aluminum industry, and of a great hydroelectric power complex with its dams, electrical generating capacity, and transmission lines. Seconded to the North East Development Company, they established a TVA-like regional development project. Seconded to the successive economic "general staffs," they did the nitty-gritty of logistical planning. They staffed the cabinet's Central Planning Board. In 1943, the Central Planning Board and MCI merged to become the Ministry of Munitions (MM). MM had among its tasks the control of stockpiles, the control of prices in strategic industries, the creation of a synthetic petroleum industry, the accelerated development of strategic industries generally, and the control of resource imports and materials allocation.

Under the mobilizations laws of 1938, the nominal powers of MM, charged with the task of converting all industry into war production, were virtually unlimited. In spite of their nominal authority, the enormity of their responsibilities, and the depth of knowledge acquired through the unmatched complexity and difficulty of tasks they had undertaken, the MCI officials did not exercise real industrial control. Crushed between the inexpert but overwhelming power of the military on the one side, and the powers of self-control exercised by the *zaibatsu* on the other, and subordinate to both, they were frustrated in their attempts at general planning or real coordination. Partly to escape the *zaibatsu*, MM established and operated a series of public corporations.

MITI Restructures the Postwar Economy

After Japan's surrender and before the Americans had taken over, the munitions ministry vanished. MCI, purged of military officers, reappeared. The army and the *zaibatsu* had dominated the economy during the years of mobilization and war. The American occupation dismantled and displaced them both; but MCI, with the great powers it had acquired as MM, was left intact. In 1952, the seven-year United States occupation of Japan ended. By then, Japan had regained its 1936 level of production. Before their departure, the Americans turned over their total control of imports and exports to the Board of Trade, which, merged with MCI, became the Ministry of International Trade and Industry (MITI). What followed with MITI at the helm was probably the most successful economic performance in recorded history.

With the Americans gone, it was MITI that allocated imported resources, capital funding, and external loans. Controlling the import of foreign technology, it protected Japanese industry from foreign domination. To facilitate exports by supplying information useful in the development of foreign markets, MITI established the Japanese External Trade Organization, operating in fifty-five countries. Through its Industry Rationalization Council, it formulated, and with suggestions no private company could afford to ignore, achieved fundamental management reforms, for example, in the adoption of policies of lifelong employment, wage and promotion standards, systematic employee training programs, and quality control.

MITI resurrected the rounded industrial communities of the *zaibatsu*, rid now of control by family ownership, with professional managers of the stripe of MITI bureaucrats in charge, each still with a trading company linked to the Japanese External Trade Association.[8]

"Through its licensing powers and its preferential financing, it winnowed the approximately 2,800 trading companies down to twenty big ones, each serving a bank-centered *keiretsu* or cartel of smaller producers, with unaffiliated enterprise assigned to a particular trading company."[9]

Japanese industry was financed through the banks that MITI had established at the center of each of those rounded industrial communities. Those banks, in turn, relied on credits extended by the Bank of Japan and the Japanese Development Bank. Loan applications were screened, and the lending was directed by MITI on targeted industries scheduled in a stage-by-stage development of the Japanese industrial structure. This led, time and again, to Japanese technological preeminence in the targeted sector; from light, labor-intensive industries, to petrochemicals and steel, to automobiles, to digitally controlled machine tools and ships, to electronics, to robots and computers, to resource-conserving, nonpolluting, and antipollution technologies, to technologies for the medical and educational sectors; with MITI always planning, coordinating, and providing a specifically tailored infrastructure with research and development support for each targeted development.

With the passage of time, with the rising wealth and, hence, the financial independence of Japanese enterprise, and with international pressures for the liberalization of Japanese trade and investment, the power balance has shifted away from MITI. Its influence in the role of "administrative guidance" has become less direct and more equivocal.[10] Nevertheless, in contrast to the years of laissez-faire, *zaibatsu* self-control, or military dominance, the record stands of Japan's economic performance when MITI was at the helm. In two short decades, industrial production increased by 1200 percent; manufacturing, by 1300 percent. An oil crisis that struck Japan more brutally than it did any other country was transcended, with Japan rising to new industrial heights. And the distribution of income was less unequal in Japan than in any other capitalist economy.

Questions and Answers

We cannot become Japanese or replicate institutions rooted in a culture that is not our own. But we can learn from the Japanese, just as they learned from us. Their experience itself is silent: it is but the raw data against which we might test our hypotheses. It remains for us to formulate the hypotheses to be tested. If we want the answers, we first must ask the questions. Such is the nature of learning.

The Positive State

What is the difference between the role of the state in Japan and its role in the United States vis-à-vis the domestic economy, particularly with respect to the corporate industrial sector?

As the actor of last resort, the American state occasionally responds to the pressure of crisis and the outcry of victims, always with the ad hoc policies of the mender and the fixer after the fact. Essentially, as far as the corporate industrial sector is concerned, the activities of the American state are peripheral; its posture is passive; its responsibilities are residual.

The Japanese state, on the contrary, is directly engaged in the activities of its corporate industrial sector. In that sector, it stands as an autonomous force and participant, one among the many, but the one among the many that speaks for the interest of the whole, the collective; for the national interest. It alone stands responsible to the nation for the survival and success of Japanese industry; for the advance of Japanese technology and the rise of its industrial productivity. There can be no question that the Japanese experience establishes the feasibility and the potentialities of a positive state.

From the experience of MITI, we learn that the state can play a positive and powerful role in promoting the advance of technology and accelerating the rise in productivity, without diminishing the significance of private enterprise and the market. The communists had to learn that one system cannot undertake to encompass the control of the whole, and survive. The United States, on the other hand, must recognize that there must be some system equipped to act positively on the problems of the whole if it is to stay afloat in the sea of international competition.

This lesson from Japan, in particular, is important to us, for we in the United States have failed to develop any facet of the state as an instrument capable of organizing, coordinating, monitoring, evaluating, supporting, or in any effective way promoting the advance of technology and accelerating the rise of productivity in the critical corporate industrial sector.

Dual Management

What is the character of the relationship between the public and the private, between MITI and corporate enterprise, in the corporate industrial sector?

The relationship is one of dual management. The agency of the state is an autonomous actor in a universe of its peers. It operates, not through coercion and command, but through leverage and influence. It differs from corporate management in being answerable to the body politic rather than to the internal control of enterprise, and in bringing public goals and social criteria into the process of choice. If it represents the nation's need and interest in the formation of industry's policies, it also represents industry's need and interest in the formation of national policy. It shares with corporate management and labor leadership the goals of rapid technological advance, higher productivity, job security, industrial profitability and growth, price stability. For MITI to achieve its own goals, it needs and will therefore promote the effective, innovative, internal management of corporate enterprise. Hence between the public agency and the private company, relationships are mostly symbiotic, and only occasionally conflicting.

There can be no question that Japanese experience establishes the feasibility and the potential effectiveness of a system of dual management for the corporate industrial sector.

The Instrument

Dual management requires an instrument for the formation and implementation of public policy, and for the effective expression of the public interest in the joint formation of corporate policies. In Japan, MITI was that instrument. Great ideas, brilliant schemes, surefire programs are mere fantasies without a high-quality instrument for their evaluation and implementation. The instrument is prior to the policies, for if such an instrument of public action is in place it will on its own evolve ideas, schemes, and programs for the task at hand.

What qualities, what competencies, what organizational character are required for, or are relevant to the formation of an instrument for the dual management of the corporate industrial sector?

Relevant, certainly, to MITI's success are the following.

1. MITI carefully recruits an intellectual elite by examination. No

silk purses will be fashioned from sows' ears, either in Japan or in the United States. Inasmuch as the educational system and competitive examinations can select, MITI selects the best of each oncoming generation. For this, there is no equivalent in the American polity.

2. Those so selected are offered careers of great honor and continuity, and a life of austerity, dedicated labor, and service, with the opportunity to rise to the very highest level of power and responsibility. The only way to that apex of economic power is through the professional ranks. No millionaire stockbrokers, or top corporate executives are brought in from the outside to run the show. For it is understood that a particular body of knowledge and skills relevant to the formation of public policy (in contrast to corporate policy), and a table of values proper to public in contrast to private or corporate choice, are acquired uniquely through a lifetime of MITI-like experience. There is no equivalent of this in the American polity.

3. The task is entrusted to a small group, no larger than a university faculty, tightly knit, self-perpetuating, possessing a high degree of independence from any other agency of the state, and broadly autonomous in the formation of policy and the choice of strategy. There is no equivalent of this in the American polity.

4. Recruits are systematically trained to shoulder the full range of MITI's responsibilities. They learn by doing. Guided, supported, and monitored by their peers, from the start they are systematically exposed to a great range of tasks, and offered opportunities for creative initiative. Their knowledge of industry and technology becomes at least as profound, their competence in management and finance, at least as great as that of those in control of the industrial entities to which their concerns relate. For this, there is no equivalent in the American polity.

5. MITI shaped itself, not only as a functional instrument, but as a living community, bound by ties of pride and loyalty, with vertical and horizontal relationships carefully cultivated, offering a secure and cherished way of life, providing the opportunity for individual self-fulfillment and an outlet for collective purpose and individual dedication. For this there is no equivalent in the American polity.

Unanswered

You and I might learn easily enough from a review of the experience of Japan. But can our society, can the American state so learn? It is in transforming itself—its ideology, its institutions, and its values—that a society learns.

Can we—would we—undertake the responsibilities of a positive state?

Can we—would we—select and recruit the top of the crop to the public service, and train them to shoulder those responsibilities and perform the tasks of a positive state?

Can we—would we—offer them a lifetime career of austerity and honor, and in order to attract the best, to capture their ambition, and to ensure that the knowledge and skills that are the cumulative residue of their singular responsibilities and experience will fully serve the public interest, can we—will we—give them the opportunity to rise through the ranks to the highest level of responsibility and power?

Can we—will we—give the independence and continuity needed to the instrumentality of positive action so that it might develop both an esprit and the competence required for its role; will we also allow it the autonomy needed for the foresightful formation and the longsighted implementation of policy so that it might effectively participate with private enterprise in the development of the corporate industrial sector?

If we cannot—or will not—what will the consequences be? What options remain?

Notes

1. A sampling of relevant publications is given in the reference list.

2. See Johnson, Chalmers. *MITI and the Japanese Miracle*. Stanford: Stanford University Press, 1982; and Gibney, Frank. *Miracle by Design*. New York: Times Books, 1982. Gibney, relying on Chalmers, takes the work of MITI into account.

3. For a discussion of the specifics of Japanese culture, see Irige, Akira. *The Chinese and the Japanese*. Princeton: Princeton University Press, 1981; Ishida, Ellchiro. *Japanese Culture*. Tokyo: University of Tokyo Press, 1974; Lebra, Takie Sugyama. *Japanese Patterns of Behavior*. Honolulu: University Press of Hawaii, 1976; and Masatsugu, Mitsuyuki. *The Modern Samurai Society: Duty and Dependence in Contemporary Japan*. New York: AMACOM, 1981.

4. For a more general discussion, see Kubota, Akira. *Higher Civil Servants in Postwar Japan*. Princeton: Princeton University Press, 1969; and Koh, B.C. *Japan's Administrative Elite*. Berkeley and Los Angeles: University of California Press, 1987.

5. Johnson, Chalmers. *MITI and the Japanese Miracle*, p. 80.

6. See also Krauss, Ellis S.; Rohlen, Thomas P.; and Steinhoff, Patricia, eds. *Conflict in Japan*. Honolulu: University of Hawaii Press, 1984.

7. See Hirschman, J., and Yu, T. *The Development of Japanese Business*

1600–1981. London: Allen and Unwin, 1981, for a longer range survey.

8. See also Mannari, Hiroshi, and Befu, Harumi, eds. *The Challenge of Japan's Internationalization*. Tokyo: Kodansha International, 1983; Yoshino, M.Y., and Lifson, Thomas B. *The Invisible Link, Japan's Sogo Shosha and the Organization of Trade*. Cambridge, MA: MIT Press, 1986; and Young, Alexander K. *The Sogo Shosha, Japan's Multi-National Trading Company*. Tokyo: Charles E. Tuttle, 1979.

9. Johnson, Chalmers. *MITI and the Japanese Miracle*, p. 206.

10. See also Hollerman, Leon. *Japan Disincorporated: The Economic Liberalization Process*. Stanford, CA: Hoover Institute Press, 1984.

References

Abegglen, James, and Stalk, George. *Kaisha, the Japanese Corporation*. New York: Basic Books, 1985.

Allen, George, C. *Japan's Economic Policy*. London: Macmillan, 1980.

———. *The Japanese Economy*. London: Weidenfeld and Nicolson, 1981.

Alston, John P. *The American Samurai: Blending American and Japanese Managerial Practice*. Berlin and New York: de Gruyter, 1986.

Bingman, Charles. *Japanese Government Leadership Management*. New York: St. Martin's Press, 1989.

Buckley, Rogers. *Japan Today*. Cambridge: Cambridge University Press, 1985.

Clarke, Rodney. *The Japanese Company*. New Haven: Yale University Press, 1979.

Cole, Robert E. *Japanese Blue Collar*. Berkeley and Los Angeles: University of California Press, 1973.

———. *Mobility and Participation: A Comparative Study of American and Japanese Industry*. Berkeley and Los Angeles: University of California Press, 1979.

Dore, Ronald. *Flexible Rigidities: Industrial Policy and Structural Adjustment in the Japanese Economy 1970–1980*. Stanford: Stanford University Press, 1986.

———. *Taking Japan Seriously: A Confucian Perspective on Leading Economic Issues*. Stanford: Stanford University Press, 1987.

Dore, Ronald, and Sako, Mari. *How the Japanese Learn to Work*. London and New York: Routledge, 1989.

Frank, Isaiah, ed. *The Japanese Economy in International Perspective*. Baltimore: Johns Hopkins University Press, 1983.

Freeman, Christopher. *Technology Policy and Economic Performance: Lessons from Japan*. Dover, NH: Francis Pinter, 1987.

Hatakeyama, Yoshio. *Managerial Revolution!* Cambridge, MA: Productivity Press, 1985.

Hayashi, Kichero, ed. *The Management of Economic Systems in the United States and Japan*. New York: New York University Press, 1988.

Hayashi, Shuji. *Culture and Management in Japan*. Tokyo: University of Tokyo Press, 1988.

Iwata, Ryushi. *Japanese Style Management*. Tokyo: Asian Productivity Organization, 1982.

Johnson, Chalmers; Tyson, Laura; and Zysman, John. *Politics and Productivity: How Japan's Development Strategy Works.* Cambridge, MA: Ballinger, 1989.

Kahn, Herman, and Pepper, Thomas. *The Japanese Challenge.* New York: Crowell, 1979.

Kelly, Allen C., and Williamson, Jeffery G. *Lessons from Japanese Development.* Chicago: University of Chicago Press, 1974.

Komiya, Ryutaro, and Okuno, Mashiro. *Industrial Policy in Japan.* New York: Academic Press, 1988.

Lee, Sang M., and Schweniman, Gary, eds. *Japanese Management: Cultural and Environmental Considerations.* New York: Praeger, 1982.

Levine, Solomon B., and Kawada, Hisashi. *Human Resources in Japanese Industrial Development.* Princeton: Princeton University Press, 1980.

McMillan, Charles. *The Japanese Industrial System.* Berlin and New York: de Gruyter, 1985.

Magaziner, Ira, and Hout, Thomas. *Japanese Industrial Policy.* Berkeley: Institute of International Studies, 1981.

Nakamuru, Takafusa. *The Postwar Japanese Economy: Its Development and Structure.* Tokyo: University of Tokyo Press, 1984.

Ochi, William. *Theory Z. How American Businessmen Can Meet the Japanese Challenge.* Reading, MA: Addison Wesley, 1981.

Pascale, Richard T., and Athos, Anthony G. *The Art of Japanese Management.* New York: Simon and Schuster, 1981.

Pepper, Thomas; Janow, Merit; and Wheeler, Jimmy. *The Competition: Dealing with Japan.* New York: Praeger, 1985.

Samuels, Richard. *The Business of the Japanese State.* Ithaca, NY: Cornell University Press, 1987.

Sasaki, Naoto. *Management and Industrial Structure in Japan.* New York: Pergamon Press, 1986.

Sato, Kazuo. *Economic Development of Japan.* London: Basil Blackwell, 1988.

Schonberger, Richard J. *Japanese Manufacturing Techniques.* New York: Free Press, 1982.

Tanaka, Hiroshi. *Personality in Industry: The Human Side of Japanese Enterprise.* Philadelphia: University of Pennsylvania Press, 1988.

Thurow, Lester, ed. *The Management Challenge: Japanese Views.* Cambridge, MA: MIT Press, 1985.

Vogel, Ezra, ed. *Modern Japanese Organization and Decision-Making.* Tokyo: Charles E. Tuttle, 1979.

―――. *Modern Japanese Organization and Decision-Making.* Berkeley and Los Angeles, University of California Press, 1989.

5 • AIM

An Instrument of Discretionary Control

Public policy in the United States with respect to its industrial economy has been expressed through the passive imposition of rules as parameters of business choice. The tasks before us, the problems we face, and the solutions we will propose here require more than that. They require that the state enter the industrial economy as an active player, to participate in the development of corporate industrial policy, to negotiate the coordination of business activity, and to influence and guide the direction of that activity. There exists now in the American government no agency organized for, or capable of, such an undertaking. The instrument of positive action is lacking.

Can we develop, in the United States, an instrument of government, operating independently but in close association with the great industrial corporations, with an experience at least as deep and an expertise at least as great as that of their management, and with a knowledge of the potentials, problems, and policies of every firm? Could such an agency serve as Congress's instrument of surveillance, bringing information and advice into the legislative process, assisting Congress in the design of legislation and the formation of industrial policies, while developing new options for its own discretionary action or for Congressional consideration? As an informed and disinterested observer interfacing industry and government, could it convey to Congress the real needs of industry, and forewarn of impending problems and crises? Especially, could it act to represent the public interest in a system of dual management in the corporate industrial sector?

MITI's character and Japanese experience were analyzed in chapter 4. Could that which is relevant to MITI's effectiveness be replicated in an American agency? Would its creation and deployment be feasible in the American context?

Is MITI a Feasible Model?

In Japan, the educational system serves to select, orient, and recruit the most able of each oncoming generation for the public service. That is not the case in the United States. Here, medicine, law, and Wall Street probably get the cream of the crop. American experience, nevertheless, as in the New Deal, the Kennedy administration, or the Peace Corps, suggests that honor, power, and the public service are powerful lures. An agency offering young Americans a career opportunity equivalent to that offered to the Japanese by MITI would attract more than its quota of high-caliber talent.

MITI offers its new recruits a secure lifetime career. With its leadership promoted from within, it offers its recruits the opportunity to rise to the highest level of power and honor. No corporate executives or displaced politicians are brought in from the outside to rule the roost. Throughout their tenure, recruits are systematically trained and monitored, "sent around the track," to acquire the values and to master a knowledge suited to their responsibilities. They are inculcated with a powerful esprit de corps and the sense of their worth and purpose. That this is feasible for an American agency is demonstrated by the fact that the offer of a lifetime career; evolved and extensive training; and experience "around the track," with leadership recruited only from within; and the opportunity to rise to the highest level of honor and power are all traditionally practiced in the officer corps of the American armed services.

MITI is broadly independent in the exercise of its discretionary authority. The experience of the American armed forces, the Federal Reserve Board, the FBI, and of course, the judiciary demonstrates the high degree of autonomy that can be obtained for a public agency in the United States. The great threat to its independence would come from corporate interests using their reach into, and control over, elements in Congress to influence or control the agency. The capacity of the agency to offset that threat would depend on the public image it establishes and the popular support it evokes. The need to establish that image and to evoke that support would itself be a salutary constraint on the operation of the agency.

It would be the tasks of Congress to articulate public goals, to delegate the powers to be exercised by the agency, and to establish the rules under which it must operate. Congress would be the watchdog, holding the agency accountable for its decisions and their consequences. But Congress cannot itself enter into the processes of industrial management any more than it can manage the specifics of military procurement. Congress cannot represent the public interest in the formation of corporate industrial policy. For that, it would have to rely on the agency and its corps of professionals.

MITI personnel have limitless work demands, and their life-style is austere. Could the same be expected of American personnel? Must high pay and a luxuriant life-style be offered as a work incentive, or to attract and keep the talented? The opposite could be argued: that in this instance, the higher the level of financial reward, the lower the level of service. There are many activities where the price that a good or service fetches on the market is, in some rough way, a measure of the relative real value to the purchaser of that good or service; hence, the motivation of the individual to obtain a higher reward for the good or service that he offers for sale is, at the same time, a motivation to offer goods and services of greater real value. There are, however, other activities whose real value is not to be graded by reference to the consumer's satisfaction with a purchased item: the work of a priest, for example, or of an academic scientist or a public servant. The dollar sign does not point them in the direction of greater social worth. All that holds them to that direction is an inner commitment to the values they ostensibly pursue. Rather, the pursuit of personal enrichment depletes, distorts, and corrupts that one, viable, motivational force. Hence, it is good if the prospect of austerity repels and weeds out those who would come to the public service for the opportunity to build career and fortune. It could be said of those drawn into the aforementioned professions for the sake of financial gain that the more talented and energetic they are, the more dangerous they will be for the integrity of the institution, for then they are more likely to control it and use it for personal enrichment.

MITI is a feasible model for an American agency and instrument of positive public action. Improbable in these improbable times, perhaps, but feasible, and ultimately, necessary. We shall assume the existence of the instrument, with its dedicated corps of civil servants sensitized to the table of social values, skilled in the processes of policy formation and the operation of our political system, and with a knowledge of technology and the context of industrial operations at least as great as the best of their industrial counterparts. For convenience, we will call it the Agency for Industrial Management (AIM).

Dual Management in the Corporate Industrial Sector

An article in the *New York Times* hails as "America's Answer to Japan's MITI" the Defense Advanced Research Projects Agency (DARPA) within the Pentagon, which has about $250 million of its 1989 billion-dollar budget earmarked to support the development of selected technologies in the corporate industrial sector.[1] DARPA is most certainly not the equivalent of MITI. It is strictly a military operation with neither MITI's purposes nor its responsibilities; its subsidies to business carry all the dangers and distortions inherent in the military support of civilian industrial research and development. Nevertheless, there are operating similarities to MITI. Within broad constraints, DARPA acts independently, with great latitude in its choice of to whom, and under what conditions, it will lend its support. Without coercive authority, it has power, nevertheless, via the leverage of the purse, to influence the behavior of industry. Hence, DARPA shares with the corporate executives responsibility for the management of a selected industry, orienting its development toward the goals of national security. While the military's goals and criteria are not those of which we speak, DARPA does provide an instance of dual management. AIM would institutionalize a general form of dual management for the corporate industrial sector.

The management of the corporate industrial sector would then have two components. Each would serve a different clientele, responding to a different table of values, with different responsibilities and powers. It would be for corporate management to operate the firm with profitability as its goal. Each corporate management would be responsible for the formation and implementation of its own competitive strategies; for the recruitment, hiring, and promotion of its own personnel; for planning and organizing its procurement; for research and development; for production; for product and process innovation, marketing, internal finance, and investment; and for the intra-enterprise distribution of income.

AIM would be committed to the survival and growth of the industry; to technological advance accelerating the rise of productivity, enabling higher real wage and income levels, and promoting international competitiveness; to the expansion of career and employment opportunities; to price stability; to equity in income distribution; to environmental quality; and to other social values.

The relationship between the two management components would be occasionally conflicting, but basically symbiotic. Each could be extremely useful to the other. Public management, answerable to the nation for the national industrial performance, needs, relies upon, and must support well-managed firms. Its plans and strategies cannot succeed without them. For the firm, on the other hand, it is of the utmost importance that social demands and public policies be filtered through an agency deeply knowledgeable about the circumstances and requisites of its operation, and able to represent its proper interests in the political arena and in the formation of public policy.

Co-participation

Part 1 of this book, in addressing the question of how to achieve full employment and price stability, proposed that the responsibilities and powers for managing aggregate spending be consolidated under a single authority. It was also proposed that such an authority, taking a page from the system of French Indicative Planning, base its policies on the actual investment plans of corporate enterprise, rather than on speculative projections, and that it attempt to modify those plans where necessary, in order to hold investment spending within acceptable boundaries. To that end, it would work through AIM as an agency that could serve as a conduit to information concerning the investment plans of every firm in the corporate industrial sector, and also as a key participant in formulating, hence potentially in revamping, their capital investment plans.

It was also argued in part 1 that there is no way to offset the threat of stagflation except through the standby capacity to influence and constrain the formation of price/wage policy in the corporate industrial sector. It would be the task of AIM to participate in the formation of corporate industrial price and wage policy, with the power to hold the price line against an inflationary spiral, while preserving the essential function of the price system, including the elimination of only marginally efficient producers under the pressure of a cost/price squeeze. AIM should have the option of allowing temporary pricing concessions to preserve those marginal producers, with the proviso that management is changed and the organization of the company is restructured.

In its role as participant in the formation of corporate industrial policy, AIM would be empowered to impose constraints on corporate choice when significant social effects were in prospect; for example, with regard to environmental quality, price stability, employment opportunity, or the transfer of corporate operations abroad.

As a co-participant in the formation of corporate industrial policy, AIM would be responsible, not to the company shareholders, but to the nation at large for the rehabilitation, survival, and sustained growth of industry in the United States, reflected in rising wage incomes and an improved quality of life. On that account, it would be obliged to monitor performance, industry by industry and great firm by great firm, and be able, in the face of poor performance and failure, to force the replacement of corporate management and to support financially a restructuring of the organization and an upgrading of the technology under the new management.

Note

1. *New York Times.* Business section, March 5, 1989, p. 1.

PART 3

HOW CAN WE REGAIN TECHNOLOGICAL PREEMINENCE AND ACCELERATE THE RISE OF AMERICAN INDUSTRIAL PRODUCTIVITY?

Memorandum

To: Reader
From: Author
Subject: How can we regain our lost technological preeminence and accelerate the rise of American industrial productivity?

1. No society in history has lost its technological preeminence as rapidly as has the United States during the past several decades. This part of the book is intended to explain that decline, and to propose the means of reversing it.

2. One major cause of America's technological decline has been change in the internal structure and organization of corporate industrial enterprise, which has progressively widened the distance between the operation of production and the locus of decision and control. Power and choice have shifted from the production engineer to the asset manipulator.

3. A number of policy options are proposed to countervail against this malaise, in variously checking, controlling, or eliminating mergers, and requiring the internal restructuring of corporate industrial enterprise. Also, recognizing that the climb to the upper reaches of corporate management is no longer up from the shop floor but now begins at the school of business, with the Master of Business Administration degree required to reach the first rung of the ladder to climb the echelons of corporate power, and recognizing that the American business school in no way trains its graduates in the organization of production or in the management of technology, we propose a change in that system of education to prepare a management cadre oriented toward and knowledgeable with respect to the process of production and the potentials of technology.

4. A second major cause of America's technological decline is the enormous diversion of America's critical resources into the military, including the bulk of its scientists and research engineers, thereby depriving the civilian economy of its source of dynamism and capacity for regeneration.

5. Since the revolutionary changes that have occurred in Eastern Europe and the Soviet Union leave no threat to American security anywhere on the horizon, it becomes feasible and even inevitable that military and related expenditures will be radically reduced and the vast resources tied to the ends of war will be released.

6. This carries with it the promise of enormous benefits, but also a very grave threat. The long economic "recovery" in the United States has been the consequence of massive increments of deficit-based public spending pumped into the aggregate expenditure stream. To suddenly eliminate that spending would precipitate a major depression spreading itself over the world. A program is proposed to reintegrate the resources released from war industry into a productive and dynamic civil economy.

7. Other policies or programs designed to accelerate the operation of the system of technological advance are proposed, among them:

a. The role of AIM in targeting and coordinating economic development.

b. A policy designed more fully to disseminate and utilize the great stores of technologically significant information produced through corporate research and development but sequestered in company files, without inhibiting the company motivation to invest in research and development.

c. The development within the American educational system of an alternative track, following the lines of the German *hauptschule,* to upscale the capabilities of American labor, to enable the climb from the workshop and the production floor to the upper echelons of corporate management, and to open the doors of production opportunity to the children of the underclass.

d. The installation of a series of development banks to serve as an alternative to Wall Street to support investment in technological innovation and the development of technology. Again a page is taken from Japan's book of experience.

e. A program to facilitate the capacity of small businesses to adapt and respond to radical change in industrial circumstances and market opportunities. It would accelerate the introduction of new science-based technologies into their operation. It would promote and coordinate their collaboration in organizing for the joint production of complex outputs, with agencies established to finance such production, and to assist in the search for and development of market opportunities.

f. The means of avoiding the overcapitalization of agricultural land values, which was at the root of the recent crisis in the American farm economy.

6 • Losing the Race

The Stake in Technological Preeminence

Nothing is as important for the modern economy as its capacity to generate technological progress, and thereby, to raise the level of its productivity. Only that can provide a steady rise in the standard of living, a distribution of income where the betterment of one need not be through the impoverishment of another, and an escape from the trap of expanding population and diminishing natural resources.

America, at the onset of World War II, and even more at the end of the war, in its technology, hence, in its industry and in the standard of living it afforded to its people, was beyond the reach, even beyond the aspiration, of every other country in the world. We could, and we did, think of ourselves as living where the sun rises and the world turns, the richest, the greatest, with the highest standard of life, the leader and the leading edge in the advance of technology, with everything to teach and nothing to learn from the others. All that has changed.[1]

We still are rich, and powerful, and the benign decades of the fifties and sixties carried us well beyond where we stood at the war's end. But no longer are we the leader and leading edge in the advance of technology. Again and again, we have been surpassed. Indeed, never in history has any country lost its preeminence in technology, in industry, and in the capacity to provide the good life for its people so rapidly as has the United States during the past several decades. For a while, our sages soothed us with the thought that all the rest, so far behind, were simply catching up. The jolting truth hit home when the technological and industrial powers of others surpassed our own, and the great bastions of American industrial strength in steel, machine tools, and automobiles faltered, and even crumbled, under the force of foreign competition.

Explanations

If one can think of a race to advance technology and raise the level of productivity, then during the post–World War II decades, the United States has been losing the race. That fact has been extensively discussed in many publications.[2] Academics propose more funds for basic research. Those who speak for business see the solution in lower corporate taxes and less government regulation. Neoclassical economists urge more trust in a free (unprotected) market. How much credence can be given to these well-worn palliatives, buttressed with massive and always indecisive statistics, when we are losing the technology race to those with higher taxes, far more government intervention, a protectionist policy, and a lesser investment in basic research and in research and development? Certainly, none of these explanations has led to the formation of any coherent policy or to any effective measure for accelerating the advance of industrial technology.

The failure to explain can be explained. Technological progress has been regarded as something that simply occurs in the environment of a free market economy. And it did occur in the environment of a free market economy, with no need for theoretical analysis or policy concern. But, while that habit of mind may account for the lack of explanations offered, it is of no help in understanding comparative performance, or in explaining the deceleration of technological progress.

The explanations we offer are tentative. We shall look at the economy from the inside, to understand something of the multiple processes that bear upon technology and productivity. We will analyze technological advance as a system that can be variously organized, examining its components and the possible constraints on its operation. In these terms, we will hypothesize causes for the technological slowdown in the United States; reasons for our losing the race. We will identify problems in the operation of the system, and propose polices to spur the pace of technological advance.

Notes

1. The book by Ira C. Magaziner and Robert B. Reich, *Minding America's Business: The Decline and Rise of the American Economy* (New York: Harcourt Brace Jovanovich, 1982) suggests something of the depth of the problem with which we are here concerned.

Magaziner and Reich have put together some relevant statistics for the period 1959 to 1980. Comparing per capita gross national products (GNP) of other countries with that of the United States, they find the Swiss GNP per capita was 57 percent of America's in 1960, and 139 percent of the American GNP in 1979; the Danish GNP per capita was 46 percent of the American in 1960, and 119 percent in 1979; the Swedish GNP per capita was 67 percent of that of the United States in 1960, and 115 percent in 1979; the German GNP per capita was 46 percent of that of the United States in 1969, and 116 percent in 1979; the Norwegian GNP per capita was 45 percent of that of the United States in 1960, and 106 percent in 1979; the Belgian GNP per capita was 44 percent of that of the United States in 1960, and 107 percent in 1979; the Luxembourg GNP per capita was 59 percent of that of the United States in 1960, and 109 percent in 1979; the French GNP per capita was 47 percent of that of the United States in 1960, and 100 percent in 1979; GNP per capita in the Netherlands was 47 percent of that of the United States in 1960, and 101 percent in 1979; Japanese GNP per capita was 16 percent of that of the United States in 1960, and 82 percent in 1979; the Finnish GNP per capita was 40 percent of that of the United States in 1960, and 92 percent in 1979; GNP per capita in the United Kingdom was 48 percent of that of the United States in 1960, and 67 percent in 1979.

That the rest of the Western world reached us, and raced ahead, is explicable in part by the magnitude of our failure to employ our manpower resources. The average unemployment during the period 1959 to 1976 was 5.4 percent in the United States, 3.3 percent in Italy, 3.2 percent in the United Kingdom, 2.4 percent in France, 1.9 percent in Sweden, 1.4 percent in Japan, and 1.2 percent in West Germany. From 1977 until the first half of 1980, with a general rise in the level of unemployment, average unemployment was 6.5 percent in the United States, 6.1 percent in the United Kingdom, 5.8 percent in France, 4.3 percent in Italy, 3.5 percent in West Germany, 2.1 percent in Japan, and 1.9 percent in Sweden.

Productivity, the most critical indicator of technological and manufacturing prowess, is measured by real output per employed worker. From 1960 to 1973, productivity increased at the annual rate of 8.9 percent in Japan, 5.4 percent in Italy, 4.7 percent in West Germany, 4.5 percent in France, and 3.2 percent in the United Kingdom, compared to an annual productivity increase of only 1.8 percent in the United States. From 1974 until 1978, with a general slowing down of economic growth, productivity increased at an annual rate of 3.2 percent in Japan, 3.0 percent in West Germany, 3.0 percent in France, 1.1 percent in Italy, 0.8 percent in the United Kingdom, and 0.1 percent in the United States.

Underlying the recent radical reduction in the level and progressivity of the income tax in the United States, allegedly in order to increase the incentive, especially of the rich, to work and invest, is the assumption that inequality in the distribution of income, while unfortunate, is necessary to promote investment and hence, the advance of technology and the increase in productivity. (Income inequality is measured by comparing the proportion of total income received by the top 10 percent and the top 20 percent of the population with the proportion of the total income received by the lowest 20 percent of the population.) But when we compare income inequalities, it appears that those countries where inequality is the greatest are those countries where productivity has increased the least. Japan, with the highest postwar rate of economic growth, has the least income inequality, and the United States, with the lowest rate of economic growth, has had the greatest income inequality. Thus, for the period between 1960 and 1976, the annual real per capita growth rate in Japan was 7.5 percent, and the post-tax income of the top 20 percent of its population was 5.2 times greater than the post-tax income of the lowest 20 percent of its population. For a comparable period, with a real annual per capita growth rate of 2.5 percent, the post-tax income of the upper 20 percent of the American population was 9.5 times greater than the post-tax income of the bottom 20 percent. The post–World War II distribution of income has been more unequal in the United States than in Japan, Spain, France, Norway, Italy, Canada, the Netherlands, Germany, Sweden, Australia, or the United Kingdom. Not only is the gap between rich and poor greater in the United States than it is in other comparable nations, but that gap is increasing rapidly. Thus, between 1978 and 1983, the proportion of the American population below the poverty level increased by approximately 50 percent. (*New York Times*, August 3, 1984)

2. Cf. Kendrick, John, ed. *International Comparisons of Productivity and Causes of the Slowdown*. Cambridge, MA: Ballinger, 1984; Baumol, William J., and McLennan, Kenneth, eds. *Productivity Growth and U.S. Competitiveness*. New York and Oxford: Oxford University Press, 1985; *White House Conference on Productivity, Report to the President of the United States on Productivity, Growth: A Better Life for America*. Springfield, VA: National Technical Information Services, Department of Commerce, April 1984; Grossman, Eliot, and Sadler, George. *Comparative Productivity Dynamics: Japan and the United States*. Houston, TX: The American Productivity Center, 1982.

7 • Some Elements of the System

The Creative Potential

I use the term "creative potential" advisedly: I mean the potential that exists in a human population to produce, search out, discover, and recognize the significance of technologically relevant information; to invent new tools, methods and devices, and new resource combinations; to discern and to recognize the hitherto unrealized significance of some physical and social relationships.

Whatever the psychic character of that raw potential, its actualization as technological advance and higher productivity will depend on elements such as the social organization through which it operates, the institutions on which it depends, and the culture at the root of motivation and choice. Thus, Joseph Schumpeter's *The Theory of Capitalist Development,*[1] unique among its peers in basing itself on the process of technological advance, never brought inventiveness, invention, or the inventor into the picture. Schumpeter's theory turned on other roles and other functions: of the innovator, of the risk taker, of the financier. The creative sparks may fly. His interest was not in the source of the sparks but with whether they would ignite a flame. That depends on the society's capacity for governance and organization. It depends on the skills, receptivity, knowledge, interests, and flexibility of its workers and managers. It depends on the culturally inculcated, interest-rooted attitudes toward, and the resistances to, innovation and novelty. It depends on the character of incentives and on built-in motivations. All these components of the system need to be taken into account in the formation of a public policy to promote technological advance. I have conceptualized that system of technological advance elsewhere.[2]

This short chapter will only illustrate the nature of relationships between the creative potential and its institutional supports and its media
of expression (in the instance, of education and science), and the expression or repression of that potential under different forms of economic organization.

The Creative Potential and Education

Education, understood as the process of teaching/learning, associated
with verbal and logical skills, and with the capacity to comprehend and
to assimilate information, certainly has to do with the realization of a
creative potential. Besides that, there is another, critical relationship of
dependence between education and the actualization of that potential.
The individual can only realize his capacities within a framework of
thought and in relation to a learned body of knowledge; whether as the
creative farmer, the creative soldier, the creative mechanic, the creative
cook, or the creative scientist. An individual may have extraordinary
capacities to conceptualize, to invent, to leap to fresh new levels of
perception, but he will not become a creative physicist unless he has
learned physics. Through education, creativity gains access to the
niches of the system. Through education, the individual finds a takeoff
point for the exercise of creativity.

The Two Systems of Science

There exist in our time two very different but related systems of science:
the science of the sort done in the universities, and the science operating under the direction and serving the purposes of large public and
corporate organizations. Both offer an outlet for the creative potential.

The former species of science is exceedingly venerable, going back
to the Golden Age of Greece, and reborn in the skepticism of the
Renaissance. Its practitioners call it "pure," "basic," "fundamental,"
and because it depends on the goodwill of private or public donors,
such self-serving terms as these are more than understandable. Still,
those of us who walk the halls of the academy know that what university research produces is rarely worth such accolades. We will call this
sort of science, simply, "academic."

Academic science operates as a remarkable set of open-ended,
world-encompassing discourses, continuous through generations,

freely entered into by individuals autonomously engaged in producing, elaborating on, and testing the credibility of information. Each has its archives, its communication networks, and its direct link to higher education. Not only does it produce a mass of information, it is also organized systematically to prune that output, to evaluate, to select, to generalize on, and to propagate that which is considered significant through the educational nexus.

The other sort of science, which operates under the direction of government and corporate organizations, is research and development.

Scientists of both sorts have mastered the same body of academic science, have acquired the same research skills, use the same apparatus of analysis to produce and verify information sought for as possibly relevant to the solution of a problem, or in finding the answer to a question. The critical difference between the two is who asks the questions they seek to answer; who determines the problems on which they focus.

The academic scientist is largely free to ask his own questions. Research and development, on the other hand, must be oriented to problems and purposes that are of concern to an employing organization, and employing organizations want technologically relevant information of practical value. Correspondingly, the information normally produced through academic science is peripheral to technology. The contrary is true of the information produced through research and development.

The information science produces is a resource of incalculable importance. It is also a resource of unique and curious characteristics. An item of information, say the calculus, produced by Jones, is of inestimable value. The same item of information subsequently produced by Smith is valueless. Nothing is as easy to steal as is an item of information. A glance at it, and it has been stolen; yet, it is never taken away from the one by whom it was initially possessed. It cannot be exhausted through use. For the incremental use of an item of information, the marginal costs are zero. This means that to optimize its value, it must be freely given to any and all who can use it; any constraint on its use will diminish its possible contribution.

A powerful motivation to publish and to disseminate freely the information produced through academic science is built into the self-interest of the academic scientists, and a world-spanning network of publications are available to facilitate that dissemination. On the contrary, corporate organizations are motivated to withhold the information produced through their research and development, except where it must be embodied in a marketed product or where it can be sold or licensed at a price. The bulk of the research and development in the United States has been for the defense agencies, which impose formidable security constraints on dissemination. Correspondingly, the contribution of research and development to technological advance is reduced.

While academic science has developed a complex system for evaluating and selecting items considered important, for generalizing on and synthesizing these, and for feeding the synthesis back into the educational nexus, nothing of the sort exists for information produced through research and development.

From the Renaissance into the nineteenth century, academic science had a glorious record of achievement in revealing the nature of our world, but it was virtually irrelevant to the advance of technology. At the same time, for this was the period of the industrial revolution, technology was taking giant strides. The industrial revolution, the founding of our great modern industrial base in railroads, steel, machine tools, rubber, and automobiles owed virtually nothing to science. During those years science did not spill over into the industrial economy. The advance of technology and the advance of science were spectacular and simultaneous, but on separate tracks.

The change came in the mid-nineteenth century under the industrialization policies of the first great modern organization: the bureaucratic Prussian state. Committed to the industrialization of a backward, rural, peasant society, it mobilized its scientists to apply their established methods and experimental models to the solution of another set of problems, to answer a different set of questions, to test statements of a different order, where problems, questions, and statements were related to the development of technology. Thus, research and development was born. That the birth of research and development was under the aegis of a great modern organization, and that the spread and magnitude of research and development increased as the economy of the large public and corporate organization replaced the economy of very numerous, small (man-sized) private entrepreneurships was no accident. It was a matter of necessity, and a demonstration of the way in which the form of economic organization affects the realization of a creative potential.

Economic Organizations
and the Creative Potential

In the economy of very numerous, small firms, owned individually, and operated by their owners, technologies are necessarily shaped within the observational scope of an owning, controlling individual. This provided an unmatched breadth of opportunity for the individual coming into the firm to learn and master a technology from top to bottom, on the job, as part of the job. It also offered opportunities of an unmatched range and breadth for the owner-operator of the firm to experiment, invent, risk, and innovate. From within the ferment of this economy of small owner-controlled enterprise, the creative potential found its outlet in an outpouring of invention. From the seeds of that invention, the great organizations of the corporate industrial economy first developed.

The coming of the economy of the large corporate and public organization closed down those creative outlets once open to every man on the job, as part of the job. Perforce, the great organization fixes the individual into a plan; the assembly line is its prototype. The function of each is fitted to the line, where individual deviation destroys the operation of the whole. In no way can the economy of great organizations provide a range of creative opportunities for the common man equivalent to that afforded by the vastly numerous, owner-operated, small firms that the great organizations had displaced. Nor can the economy of great organizations offer an equivalent opportunity to learn by doing, as in the small firm, where the individual, from any point of operation, could observe and comprehend a whole technology.

Because it was necessary to replace the spontaneous technological learning and the independent inventive activity that had been possible in an economy of small enterprise, the learning of technology was incorporated into the system of higher education; research and development at the top replaced the upswelling of invention from the bottom. A small elite of science-trained professionals, drawing on the archive and using the methods of science, was systematically engaged in the planning and organization of technological advance.

Research and development was incorporated, naturally enough, into the core of those science-based industries spawned by the science laboratory, for example, chemicals, plastics, pharmaceutics, and electronics. For those others, like railroads, steel, automobiles, and machine tools, research and development has come slowly, if at all.

Issues

This chapter has introduced, in a very general way, some of the elements of the system of technological advance and economic progress. Hopefully, this will convey the complexity and the multifaceted character of the system where the forms of education, the varieties of science, the culture, the structure of power, the scale of enterprise, the organization of industry, the business ethos, the sources of finance, the management of information, and product outlets and demands are integral to its operation, or bear upon its processes. What follows will analyze such elements in their concrete American context.

We turn, first, to the business ethos, management practice, and structure and organization of corporate enterprise in the United States.

Notes

1. Schumpeter, Joseph. *The Theory of Capitalist Development.* Cambridge, MA: Harvard University Press, 1934.
2. See Solo, Robert A. *Economic Organizations and Social Systems.* Indianapolis: Bobbs Merrill, 1967, ch. 6–14, 22, 24, 27, 30, 34.

8 • Decline of the American System

The American System of Industrial Management

There is some dispute as to whether the modern corporation can be understood as a rational, profit-maximizing entity. Let us assume that it can be. But the mode and technique of management and the form and structure of organization that would maximize profits in these vastly complex organizations remain open questions. Answers have depended on a set of perceptions developed over generations that we might call the paradigm of industrial management. That paradigm, evolving from the onset of the industrial revolution, achieved a kind of culmination in early twentieth-century America in what has been called the ''American system'' of industrial management.

The American system included the commitment (associated with the theories of Adam Smith)[1] to specialization and standardization with the concomitant need for access to mass markets. It included the commitment to mechanization, substituting mechanical for human energy, and the dexterity of the machine for that of the human hand, with the concomitant concentration of wealth required to amass series of machines so that they might be efficiently maintained and operated as integral processes.[2] With this, the modern industrial corporation evolved as a gigantic self-financing device, and the institutional basis for a boundless concentration of assets and expansion of operations.

Our native contribution to the formation of the American system was in the ''scientific management'' associated with the work of Frederick Winslow Taylor[3]: disciplining labor into the rhythm and

79

rationale of the machine, as if workers were themselves machines. Each worker, and the movements of each worker, were to be planned, designed, and fitted into an encompassing, integral but multifaceted scheme, with the whole to be designed, planned, and experimentally developed by engineers whose education, training and experience equipped them for that task. There was to be no individual initiative, no thinking about the work by those on the job on the shop floor. Thinking must be kept apart from working; at every level, it was the task of those above systematically to de-skill and to routinize, hence better to plan, supervise, and control the work of those below.

Taylorism had, perhaps, a relevance and value particular to the process of industrialization as he saw it occurring in early twentieth-century America when immigrants from the deeply primitive peasant life of Ireland, Eastern Europe, southern Italy—illiterate, ignorant, brutalized, raw—flocked to the mills of our industrial valleys. Arguably, in order to be drawn into the operations of modern industry, they had to be subordinated and directed, worked under an iron rule, fitted into controlled routines.

This system served us well. During the decades before World War II, operating in the vast, expanding, and highly protected domestic market, it raised American wealth and power beyond the reach of any other nation. It was flawed, nevertheless these flaws would become the seeds of its decline.

Rigidities

The post–World War II decades witnessed an increasingly affluent consuming public giving greater emphasis to variety and quality than to price; the United States emerging from its hitherto protected domestic economy into the world trading system, confronting American industry with a new diversity of demands while a new range of product varieties were introduced into the American market from abroad.

The American system at its best, with its massive array of machines narrowly vectored to the continuous, high-volume production of standardized items at the lowest possible cost, was ill-equipped to meet the new need for flexibility, high quality, and product variation.

Labor's Bind

Under the American system, workers worked by the rule. Each task was prespecified, broken into its time and motion components, studied, designed, and imposed by rule. The worker was manipulated just as machines were in a practice that (a) created a permanent relationship of aggressive pressure and defense between labor and management and (b) offered workers no outlet for creativity in their labor.

Collective bargaining developed in this context of task specification and work rule. What had been the worker's obligation, now became his right, his turf. Task and rule, codified in labor agreements, endlessly elaborated in grievance procedures and work disputes, further rigidified the system, making it harder still to introduce innovation or otherwise to deviate from established modes of production.

If market demand, resource availability, and technology are all given, the Taylorite subordination and control of labor might well be the best way to produce a particular product at the lowest possible cost. But when resource availabilities and market demands are not given; when the demand and the cost context are shifting and variable, when it is essential to change, adapt, and innovate; when technology must be continuously transformed and creatively deployed; then the task is to ease the path to change and to tap creativity, expertise, and cooperative initiative wherever it can be found.

In early twentieth-century America, F.W. Taylor described laborers as "more or less the type of an ox,"[4] and there is certainly no initiative or creativity to be tapped from the yoke of oxen. In our time, the creative potential of labor is not so easily dismissed. The modern work force can be sophisticated, literate, and in matters of inventiveness and creativity, at least the equal of management. It has, besides, a more direct knowledge of, and experience in, operations. The American system stifled initiatives from below.

This top-down control and discipline of the American system not only deprived the American economy of the initiatives and creative contributions of its industrial work force; it also deprived the work force of an outlet for its ingenuity and creativity; it deprived the worker on the shop floor of opportunity for the camaraderie, the small triumphs, the sense of meaning the ego craves. In their dumb, rule-defined enclaves, alienated generations of labor were restless with suppressed ambitions and energies, not only not assisting, but resisting, innovations and transformations that must, in some way, threaten their small rule-bound turf of work and security.

The Reform of Corporate Industrial Practice

These flaws have been variously attacked by the critics of the American system. During the 1980s, under the catalyst of Japanese success, taking Japanese practice as its model, American industry launched a much-heralded phase of corporate reform from within.[5] The evidence of change is not yet in. We reserve judgment as to what initiative of the American state might be required to promote the transformation of the American management system.

There are other serious flaws of industrial structure that cannot be reached through internal corporate reform.

The Pathology of Hierarchism

Taylor supposed that the "thinking" would be done by the industrial engineer of the "planning and laying out department," trained and specialized in the organization and coordination of work, the design of technology, the simplification of work tasks, the integration of labor into the discipline and rhythms of the machine, and the formulation of rules at the level of operations.[6] Taylor's approach glorified the role of the engineer. There was, however, yet another locus of corporate values, skills, and power.

As corporate enterprise in the United States expanded and deepened, multiplying the operations within its scope, following the rule that thinking should be done from above, with operations below fixed into routines that could be effectively supervised and controlled from above, the industrial engineer was superseded and his skills devalued. As operations proliferated and tasks diversified, other managements designed to control procurement, marketing, recruitment, and promotion overlaid and controlled the domain of the industrial engineers. When operations were consolidated into divisions, new layers of control were superimposed; when divisions were consolidated into subsidiaries, other layers still. When subsidiaries were internationalized and spread over the globe, again a layer upon the layers of management and control was added. Each new level of management worked to simplify, de-skill, routinize, and hence, more completely control that which was subordinate to it.

With each stage in this expanding and deepening of the scope of corporate enterprise, with managerial echelon built upon managerial echelon in a rising hierarchy of power, the distance between the working and the thinking widened; the distance between the shop floor, where the goods were produced, and the locus of direction, discretion and power widened. That distance was crammed with clerical, service, and administrative personnel whose numbers increased as the proportion of those engaged in production diminished. The higher the ratio in the number of those engaged in administration to the number of production workers (hence, the greater the distance between the production base and the power apex), the slower became the rise in productivity.[7]

The managerial echelons moved upward, but toward what? Who held the highest status, who were most richly rewarded, who exercised the greatest power, at the summit of the corporate hierarchy? They were not the production engineers, the research scientists, those who designed new products and processes, or the masters of technology; those at the apex managed not operations, but assets, finance, the investment and disinvestment decisions to which all else was subordinated. They were the golden boys of the hierarchy. Respect and ambition throughout were pointed in their direction, oriented away from the zone of technical responsibility toward the zone of asset manipulation. Higher education followed suit. A new breed from the universities, their M.B.A. degrees in hand, were trained and indoctrinated to populate those upper reaches of the hierarchy, knowing nothing of production or technology, removed entirely from, and wholly disinterested in, the organization of operations.

In the nineteenth century Karl Marx postulated a conflict of classes: between the proletariat, who worked in industry, and the capitalist, who financed industry. He predicted that the working class must triumph because they had the knowledge and skill that counted. He was mistaken. At the turn of the twentieth century, Thorstein Veblen postulated another struggle for corporate industrial control: between those who organized production and those who manipulated assets, that is, between the engineer and the financier. He predicted the triumph of the organizer of production because the engineer had the knowledge and skill that counted. He, too, was mistaken. The engineer would be shunted aside. In the American corporate context, all the high cards were dealt to the asset manipulator. This structural distortion of the American system was not allowed to happen in Japan.

In the crucial conflict that Thorstein Veblen foretold, the money man, the asset manipulator, has left the production engineer in the dust. Such was what William J. Abernathy, Kim B. Clark, and Alan M. Kantrow called the "maturation" of enterprise,[8] wherein the earlier emphasis on process, on the fundamentals of technology, and on basic innovation gives way to gimmickry and cosmetics, which is, as far as the development of production is concerned, all that falls within the scope of the asset manipulator's comprehension and judgment.

Even assuming that profit maximization is the goal of the corporate industrial entity, there are many different paths toward that goal. Whether or not they succeed in maximizing profits, some of those paths are in the public interest; others are not. It is our hypothesis moreover that the paths chosen will depend on the knowledge, skills, and interests of those who exercise the power of choice; hence, that which distances corporate leadership from the experience of the shop floor will correspondingly divert the path of corporate development from the organization of production and technological innovation, thereby reducing the power of enterprise to generate technological progress and to raise the level of productivity.

The ultimate distortion of the American corporate industrial structure is yet to be told. It is a distortion that has its roots in the particular application of American antitrust law.

Conglomeration

Until the end of World War II, the American Supreme Court would not allow the prosecution of mergers under the antitrust laws. After World War II, that constraint was removed. The Department of Justice and the Federal Trade Commission engaged in a long series of successful attacks on horizontal mergers (where merging companies served the same market) and vertical mergers (where merging companies had some raw material–end product link). These mergers were attacked because, it was believed, they might harm competition. On the other hand, these horizontal and vertical mergers could have a positive value in achieving economies of scale, in minimizing transaction costs, and in a more efficient organization of production.

The barrier to horizontal and vertical mergers imposed by the antitrust agencies did not slow down the merger movement, but it did change its character. The energies and ambitions of corporate elites flowed into the channel that remained open, namely, into mergers between companies that had neither markets nor technologies in common, companies without horizontal or vertical linkage; hence, where there was no overt threat to competition, but also where there could be no technological or organizational rationale for merging. Such conglomerate mergers were encouraged by antitrust lawyers and economists as "acquiring footholds."

Of the mergers that took place between 1948 and 1951, some 62 percent were horizontal or vertical, and the rest could be rationalized as product extensions. In 1968, 90 percent of mergers were conglomerates,[9] divorced from any conceivable technological or organizational rationale or value; nor were they conceivably part of a strategy intended to secure a position of monopoly power. Mergers, takeovers, and buy-outs became ends in themselves. Conglomeration became a mode of business, a way of life; a perfect environment for the asset manipulator.

Conglomeration could not fail to create a universe of technological and organizational monstrosities, that is, operations flung together without technological or organizational rationale. Conglomeration was the ultimate triumph of the money man over the production engineer. After conglomeration, there was no way that those exercising control from the top could possess a knowledge of the shifting kaleidoscope of diverse and unrelated technologies at the base. Hence, there was no way that the ruling corporate elites could evaluate or competently promote the risky but essential long-range development of the technologies in their charge. After conglomeration, there was no way that those with the power of choice could possess the experience and insight required to select the best from among the many and diverse avenues of research and technological development.

After conglomeration, there emerged a corporate power elite of strategic planners, financial wizards, asset manipulators, stock promoters, Wall Street tricksters, buy-out artists, legal eagles, and stock raiders. Quicksilver loose and fancy-free, they were in no sense concerned with, or engaged in, the processes of production, the development of technologies, or anything that contributes to our standard of life. Their aim was to skim the cream without attending to, without even milking, the cow. They are the opposite of the company man. A company, their company, any company is not, and cannot be for them a living community of which they feel a part; to which they are committed; where they are rooted. The company is just a chip in the game they play; a thing to be traded; an object of takeover, to be bought and sold, drained and depleted. This has its consequences.

Given their brief and transitional tenure, their ignorance of technology, and their indifference to the specifics of operation, the organization of work, the long-range planning for industrial renewal, the development and installation of innovational technologies, and the transgenerational renewal of labor skills all go by the board. Total emphasis is on the quick fix, the fast turnover, immediate profits (the "bottom line"); payoffs to themselves and their clients gained through their indubitable skills in paper entrepreneurship and asset manipulation. Thus, the American paradox of which Seymour Melman speaks: "profits without production"; rising profits and a declining economy, with executive rewards greater than in those countries that have, by the measure of production and productivity and the rise in wage income, shown us their dust.

There is a parallelism with the path of British industrial decline: a social bifurcation akin to that which occurred in English society during the nineteenth and early twentieth centuries, coupling immense wealth at the top with industrial neglect and decay, where the ruling class derived its untaxed income from its accumulated overseas investments and from dealings in "the City" as the world center of international finance. So, also, our new executive class has detached itself from the organizing of production, and hitched its star to transnational transactions and the floating universe of asset manipulation and paper entrepreneurship. In both the American and the British instances, the self-interest of those who rule in their domestic economy is primarily as consumers, hence in low-priced goods and cheap services. Industrial degradation and whatever depresses wages and promotes the servility of labor redounds to their advantage.

From our perspective, the mortal sin is in a restructuring of industry that has destroyed the possibility of a technologically knowledgeable, innovation-oriented leadership from above, as earlier the management structure stifled creative initiatives from below. What is to be done?

Life without Mergers

Corporate mergers have become so commonplace, so numerous, so much the grist of financial and business reporting, that one might suppose that mergers are necessary for the market to function and for business to perform. Nothing could be further from the truth. Indeed, we might inquire: Have mergers any value? Why not forbid them entirely, or tax the process so heavily that merging would become a rare event?

It is demonstrably true that professionals variously engaged in the now highly evolved process of merger (or takeover, or buy-out) have established lucrative careers and accumulated vast fortunes without adding anything at all, not a single good or service, to the national product. For them, mergers have a most tangible worth. Our concern, however, is with the value of mergers to society. What do they add to or subtract from the operation of the market and the performance of business enterprise?

Without mergers, businesses can and do grow within their established markets. Without mergers, businesses can and do extend their operations forward into end products, and backward into the production of supplies and raw materials. Without mergers, they can and do diversify, establishing operations in other markets. They can and they will continue to grow in size, to integrate horizontally and vertically, and to diversify when there are real and realizable advantages in so doing, *without mergers*. Alternatively, businesses can expand, integrate operations backward or forward, and diversify through mergers. The difference is this: Without the merger option, in order to expand for any purpose and in any direction, the firm must increase the intensity of competition; it must pass the test of competition; it must offer a preferred, lower cost, higher quality good or service. For that, management must master the relevant new technologies. Nothing of the sort is to be associated with expansion through merger. If competition is the dynamic force for efficiency and progress in the corporate industrial economy, then merger, as a deviation from the path of competition, debilitates that dynamic force. On that account, given a belief in the efficacy of competition, the total elimination of mergers would upgrade the market function and improve the operation of business enterprise. It is difficult to see how mergers of any sort yield benefits of any sort to society.

Our emphasis has been on a peculiarly pernicious form of merger: the conglomerate, a form of expansion that is not conceivable when growth or expansion is achieved through competitive struggle. It brings under an integral control the unrelated technologies of formerly independent entities, without production or distribution linkages in a pure design for operating inefficiency and confusion. The conglomerate form, dominant in the United States since the 1960s, tears from the merger movement its former mask of economic rationality, for it cannot be explained as seeking the economies of scale, the efficiencies of vertical integration, even monopoly power. Unrelated to any of these, the merger movement, proliferating an endless stream of organizational monstrosities, is revealed for what it is: an enormous, all-enveloping, incredibly wasteful game of asset manipulation. It absorbs all the energies of corporate leadership into the strategies of external aggression and defense, with operations pushed to the sidelines and the tasks of production and distribution forgotten. It distorts entrepreneurial perspective and widens the distance between control and production beyond the point where control can be in any way competent to engage in the long-range development of technology. It introduces a new dimension of uncertainty into the business calculus and of instability into the business context. The colossal struggle for the control of the economy between the financier and the engineer, which Thorstein Veblen foretold, has reached an absurd culmination, with the engineer steamrolled into the dust by the force of conglomeration; but the face of the victor is not so much that of the classic financier as it is that of the river gambler, the con man, the shyster, and the dealer in inside information. With those who occupy the upper echelons of the corporate hierarchy uninterested in and without knowledge of the numerous and disparate technologies within their grasp, the systematic long-range development of technological innovation becomes unthinkable, putting a closure on possibilities of technological advance.

As a single example of the waste and the burden that the merger game imposes on corporate industrial performance, consider the commonplace use of the so-called junk bonds in the strategies of takeover. Suppose company A plans to take over company B. For that purpose, it sells $1 billion worth of its bonds to banks, and uses those funds to buy a block of B's common stock, with that block of stock offered as security on the bonds. The bonds are risky. B's common stock might fall in value. The takeover attempt might fail. Hence, the banks demand and receive a very high rate of interest. A, using the leverage of the shares it has purchased, does take over B. The merged company A/B now carries an additional high interest obligation of $1 billion of junk bond debt. Now, suppose the merged A/B obtains another $1 billion through the sale of junk bonds for the takeover of company C.

The new, merged company A/B/C now bears the burden of the interest and repayment obligation on $2 billion in junk bond debt. Suppose company E, following the same strategy, with $4 billion floated in high-interest–bearing junk bonds, takes over A/B/C. The merged company A/B/C/E would bear the interest and repayment obligation for a $6 billion junk bond debt.

One cannot object to corporate borrowing when the borrowed funds are used to procure something (equipment, technology, materials, real estate, buildings) that adds to the income-producing capacity of the company. But here we have a massive accumulating debt, where the borrowed funds have not been used to purchase a single item of capital equipment or anything else that would add to the productive capabilities of the firm or of the economy. They are simply an incident in the merger game.

Anti-Merger

Remedies? A first step surely is to limit or eliminate mergers. For this there arc numerous options:

Forbid all mergers, or at least mergers between companies of a certain size.

Forbid hostile takeovers.

Allow mergers only at AIM's discretion, where a positive social contribution can be established.

Discourage the takeover game, raising the cost of asset manipulation by taxing mergers or by reducing the creditor priority of junk bonds in the bankruptcy court, or through regulation forbidding loans on junk bonds.

Future mergers would be stopped. What of the distortions already inflicted on the corporate industrial sector? As corporations have conglomerated, corporations could, under public direction, deconglomerate. This would not be entirely unprecedented. The first Securities and Exchange Commission, during the New Deal Administration of Franklin D. Roosevelt, did something similar with the immense holding company empires that controlled America's public utilities before the Great Depression. A mandatory limit was imposed on the permissible number of holding company tiers, and the entire industry was restructured into geographically coherent and technologically viable units. Correspondingly, for the modern conglomerate, a mandatory limit could be imposed on the number of distinctive technologies allowable within a single corporate control, with AIM participating to insure that the required corporate restructuring produced a series of technologically viable, organizationally coherent sets.

Anti-Antitrust

There is overlap and, perhaps, conflict among some of the tasks we have proposed for AIM; for example, with respect to mergers and the present administration of the antitrust laws under the Department of Justice and the Federal Trade Commission. Here, we would argue that, supposing industrial policy has as its purpose and justification to upgrade the level of economic performance, the approach currently embodied in the antitrust laws is profoundly flawed, at least as far as the corporate industrial sector is concerned, for the following reasons. It operates as a system for the punishment of crime. The task of accelerating the pace of technological advance and the rise of productivity is not a matter of avenging crime and punishing the criminal. It has to do with the structure and dynamic of a complex economy, where the organization and control of operations, the financial and institutional infrastructure of the business community, and the evolutionary development of corporate industrial policies are at issue. These are matters that fall outside the training, experience, interest, and inclination of the lawyers in charge at the Antitrust Division of the Department of Justice and at the Federal Trade Commission. What is the industrial structure they seek to impose? For that, their only reference model, supplied to them by academic economics, is of "pure competition," a standard so unattainable as to be irrelevant to corporate industrial enterprise, or that of "workable competition," a standard so vague and equivocal as to be meaningless. Nor does the process of adjudication enable those engaged to learn from their experience. It is a system that never looks back, and it is in no way accountable for its errors. It is concerned with winning cases, without ever inquiring as to the consequences of its victories, never asking, "What happened then?" The responsibilities for industrial policy, including the discretionary enforcement of the antitrust laws, should be shifted to an agency, such as AIM, with the task specifically of upgrading industrial performance, that would be obliged to confront and learn from its failures.

A Policy for Small Enterprise

The American economy is not of a piece. It includes a number of subeconomies, each with operating rules and problems particular to itself, and each requiring a different policy approach. The system of dual management is feasible only for the relatively few very large entities of the corporate industrial sector. There remains a vast and heterogeneous residual of small enterprise, where the full control of operations is within the reach and command of the individual owner-entrepreneur. This would include independent manufacturers producing end products for national and international markets, craft-based operations like home construction in narrowly segmented local markets, and great numbers of contracting and subcontracting satellites of corporate-industrial operations. For firms such as these, there are no control points for the determination (hence, for the codetermination) of business policy. But an agency such as AIM could design for and install in that sector systems to advance technology and raise productivity.

Since this universe of small enterprise itself consists of numerous subeconomies, let us take, as one example, the many small and medium-size firms that work as contractors and subcontractors to large industrial corporations, subordinated to, working for, geared into, and dependent upon the operations of a particular corporate industrial center. Their product is designed by that corporate industrial center. Their production is coordinated through corporate industrial procurement. The great number of bits and pieces that numerous suppliers have separately produced are assembled at the corporate industrial center into integral, marketable and marketed end products. The narrowly specialized small firms that supply and service the corporate industrial center lack the capacity to coordinate the many diverse skills and operating capabilities in combinations required to produce alternative products for other markets.

Consider the many thousands of tool and die makers, machine shops, and parts manufacturers who supply and service the great automobile companies in the American Midwest. For generations the auto companies have been their hub, their production outlet, their design center, their financial base. They have been as tied to that hub and as dependent upon it as has the worker on the assembly line. But now there is trouble and uncertainty at the auto-making hub into which they

are linked and upon which they depend. The technological preeminence of the auto companies is gone; their future is uncertain; their
production centers have scattered; they import major components and even
whole autos from Japan; they shift production out of the Midwest to use
cheap, low-grade labor abroad. And if the auto-making hub diminishes
or vanishes, what will replace it as the organizing center for those
thousands of midwestern contractors, subcontractors, and suppliers?

I have seen their operations in small towns, quasi-agricultural communities in Michigan, drawing upon a stable, rooted, disciplined supply of labor, possessing a diversity of skills and production
capabilities. Could we facilitate the flexibility and mobility of small
firms such as these in adapting to such radical change in industrial
circumstance and market opportunity as they have encountered? It
could be done by that which would enable them to work together in
combining their different production capabilities, tools, and skills to
manufacture a different product line in response to new market opportunities; and by searching out and developing those new market
opportunities at home and abroad, suitable to their production potential, working independently or in cooperation with others; and by providing development financing for multi-firm participation in
collaborative efforts to redirect production into new markets. Their
flexibility and production potential could be increased as well by open-
ing channels for the introduction of science-based technologies into
their operation, since small firms in traditional industries generally lack
the capacity to undertake the tasks of research and development, or to
exploit emerging science-based opportunities, or independently to evaluate and incorporate science-based technologies into their operations.

A Proposal

Under the aegis of AIM, complementary groups of small firms (complementary in the sense that their operations could conceivably be
combined in producing a variety of end products) would organize as
voluntary associations. As in Japan, a development bank would be
assigned to finance the coordinated operations and the capital investment required for the coordinated operations of the firms in the association. Each association would have three critical components: (1) a
trading company, (2) a coordinating center, and (3) a research and
educational center.

With an exact knowledge of the production potential of the associated group, the task of the trading company would be to search out and provide sales outlets for the end products produced or that could be produced through the combined efforts of the members of the association. The trading company would promote the wares, and act as the contracting and bargaining agent of the associated group in dealing with other corporate industrial procurement centers, with the Pentagon in defense contracting, with large marketing companies like Sears, Montgomery Ward, or K Mart, with wholesale and retail outlets, and with purchasers in foreign countries.

The development bank, working with the trading company, basing its risk assessment on the reliability of buyers, on the nature of the bargains made and the contracts entered into, and on the established capacities of those entering into the collaborative arrangement, would finance the operation and the procurement of the required supplementary equipment.

Contracts would be made, not with individual firms, but with the association's coordinating center, and the coordinating center would be responsible to the contractee for its fulfillment. Normally, one of the participating firms would assume the role of prime contractor, with other participants acting as subcontractors. It would be the task of the coordinating center to bring together participating operations, to assist in production planning and scheduling, to ensure quality control, and to test and approve the final product.

The research and educational center would be the antennae of the association, sensitized to world developments in science and technology that might be of value to the operations of the group. Where appropriate, it would modify and adapt new technology to the operating circumstances and interests of the group. It would introduce technologically relevant information by circulating publications, offering or arranging seminars and demonstrations, and providing pilot plants for hands-on learning and experimentation, in order to enable firms to acquire the mastery of new, emerging, and advanced technologies (e.g., in cryogenics, amorphous metals, or numerically controlled machine tools). It would offer or arrange for courses in management techniques and quality control, and promote the sharing of operating experience. It would develop as an information source able to respond to the queries of its clients and to assist them in overcoming problems of technology and operations.

The successful association would soon be self-supporting, with an income based on a share of the profits of operations, servicing charges, and membership assessments.

In formulating this proposal we have drawn upon the experience of (1) the Japanese *keiretsu,* communities of small enterprise, each with a development bank to finance its industrial ventures and a trading company to develop market linkages between its existing or latent production potentials and sales opportunities throughout the world; with clusters of these *keiretsu* linked to a national agency that promotes and facilitates the international marketing of all Japanese exports; (2) the state-sponsored cooperative research associations established industry by industry in Germany, France, the United Kingdom, and other countries; (3) the network of experiment stations and the extension service that generates and carries technologically relevant information to the American farmer; (4) former artisan shops in central Italy, which, having acquired a knowledge of modern technology during a phase of subcontracting for corporate industrial producers in Milan, with state support entered into a stage of collaborative end product production that has been at the heart of the economic upsurge in Italy;[10] and (5) the operation in the Netherlands of the *Bouwcentrum* as a professional information source for builders, and the establishment of the plastic industry in the Netherlands through making available the use of pilot plants to small private industry for hands-on learning and experiment.[11]

Policy for Agriculture

It has been the purpose of this chapter to formulate and propose policies that might reverse America's industrial decline. Relative to the rest of the world, American agriculture has not been in a state of relative decline. On the contrary, for the past half century, at least until the 1980s, it has been the star performer of the American economy.

Agriculture, or at least the decentralized and price-directed farm economy, approximates the pure competition idealized by laissez-faire liberalism. But, as agriculture is the most purely competitive, it is also the most completely socialized sector of the American economy. Agricultural economists like to attribute the success of the farm economy to a threefold intervention by the American state, dating from the 1860s, which took the form of (1) land grant colleges dedicated to the teaching of scientific agriculture, which developed a receptivity on the part of the independent farmer to the information produced through scientific research; (2) national and regional agricultural research centers dedicated to the development of the agricultural sciences and technologies, and of experiment stations in the land grant colleges geared to the solution of problems specific to the regional agriculture; and (3) extension services that reached every nook and cranny of rural America to link science and research to on-the-farm application and problem solving.

Although these three components of a system of technological advance in agriculture were in place before the turn of the twentieth century, the advance of productivity in American agriculture lagged far behind that in manufacturing until the 1930s, when the New Deal administration of Franklin Roosevelt set a floor under the prices of key agricultural commodities. This completed and made viable the system of technological progress.

Not only did the state develop the information, and disseminate the knowledge prerequisite to the installation of new technology; it also guaranteed a minimum price for the product of that technology, thereby encouraging investment in its installation. For the first time, the farmer could borrow and invest without the perennial fear, regardless of the success of the new technology, that a price collapse would render him unable to repay the debt incurred in installing it, and thereby cause him to lose his farm. With stabilized future pricing, the rational forward planning of private investment in agriculture became possible. From that point on, American agriculture took off for decades of extraordinary technological progress.[12]

More recently, the farm economy has run into hard times. Paradoxically, the root of the trouble is in the high productivity and high profits; hence, high rents and high land values generated by decades of technological advance. When an older generation retired to bask somewhere in the southern sun, they took with them the capitalized value of the higher productivity of their land. The succeeding generation purchased that land at a price that gave no margin for comfort. The steady rise in land values incited speculative land purchasing, not for the income that could be earned through its cultivation, but in anticipation of a further rise in its market value. Those purchases further accelerated the boom. The market value of the land came greatly to exceed the capitalized value of the income that could be earned through its cultivation.

Caught in the speculative fever, farmers borrowed at high rates of interest to increase their ownership of this overcapitalized land, and had no difficulty in servicing their swollen debt through new borrowing, as long as the value of their equity could be equated to the continuing inflation of land values.

Then, the Federal Reserve Board's monetary cure for inflation began to work. A major recession reduced consumer purchases of farm products at home, and a massive influx of foreign funds, buying dollars to invest at the very high rates of interest imposed by the monetary authority, raised the value of the dollar in relation to foreign currencies. This made the imports from the United States more costly, and reduced the demand for American farm commodities in foreign markets. Farm prices sagged. Land values collapsed. Farm foreclosures became endemic. The pressure was on to save the farmer. That seemed to mean not simply to provide an income sufficient to ensure a good life for those who worked the land, but to provide prices and a level of income sufficient to service an enormous accumulated debt.

Thus this strange prospect: Given our present property arrangements, the values of a successful agricultural program in raising farm productivity and farm income will be capitalized and siphoned off with each sale of the property; hence, the current farm generation will always be left skating on thin ice, at the edge of disaster. I know of no solution save the expropriation of land rents that Henry George proposed long ago.[13] There is a secondary problem: that of the massive use of borrowed funds for the speculative purchase of *overcapitalized* land. About that, something can be done. The banks, especially those set up by the government to serve the farm community, which, in any case, operate by reference to standard formula, should be required to base farm loans, not on the market value of the land, but only on reasonable income-earning expectations through its cultivation.

Notes

1. Each stage in the evolution of this paradigm has had its witnesses. In the eighteenth century, Adam Smith saw in industrial specialization the potential for a vast increase in productivity as the path to national wealth and power. Specializations required large-volume markets for the outputs of the specialists. Smith argued for the international freedom of trade precisely because that would enable the benefits of specialization.

2. Karl Marx was, of course, the critical witness to this phase in the

paragigm's development. To procure the massed machines and sustain their operation was costly, and had to be financed. In the political and economic context of the time, financing could come only from individuals of great wealth. Enter the capitalist. Here, Marx saw dichotomy and conflict. The product of industry would be divided between the workers who needed access to the machines and the capitalist who owned the machines, and controlled that access. In the struggle between capital and labor for the product of industry, as Marx saw it, the capitalist ruled, and the worker submitted.

3. Taylor, Frederick W. *Shop Management*. New York: Harper and Bros., 1911.

———. *The Principles of Scientific Management*. New York: Harper and Bros., 1911.

4. *Principles of Scientific Management,* p. 137.

5. See Bushnell, Paul T. "Transformation of the American Manufacturing Paradigm." Ph.D. diss., Michigan State University, East Lansing, 1988, for an excellent coverage of the reform movement from its incipiency.

6. Taylor, Frederick W. *Shop Management*, pp. 98, 99.

7. Cf. Melman, Seymour. *Profits without Production*. New York: Alfred Knopf, 1983.

8. Abernathy, William J.; Clark, Kim B.; and Kantrow, Alan M. *Industrial Renaissance*. New York: Basic Books, 1983.

9. Solo, Robert A. *The Political Authority and the Market System*. Cincinnati: South-Western, 1974.

10. See Sabel, Charles F. *Work and Politics*. Cambridge: Cambridge University Press, 1982.

11. Solo, Robert A. *Organizing Science for Technology Transfer in Economic Development*. East Lansing: Michigan State University Press, 1975.

12. The state also, in the positive action of Roosevelt's New Deal administration, financed and managed the implementation of major technological transformations. Its Rural Electrification Administration, operating through the farmers cooperatives that it sponsored and financed, spearheaded the electrification of rural America. Its Tennessee Valley Authority developed as a model instrument to promote and coordinate the multifaceted changes required for regional development. Moreover, the Army Corps of Engineers has, from its early years, engaged in the building of dams and waterworks for the irrigation of arid lands.

More than any other group in our society, the farmers owe their high productivity to the intervention of the American state. More than any other group in American society, the farmers have been subsidized at taxpayers' expense, not only in the aforementioned interventions, but also in the maintenance of the rural infrastructure.

Yet, American agriculture is the stronghold of hard-nosed conservatism. Receiving more from the public purse, depending more on the intervention of the state, than any other sector of the economy except the military industrial complex, the farmers are the truest of the true believers in libertarian laissez-faire. This paradox can be explained by the difference between the experiences with a system and the experience of the individual who occupies a niche in the system. The individual takes the system as given; he did not create it; he does not direct it; he does not identify with it or comprehend it. He is aware of it only when it rubs and rasps at the margins of his niche. But the niche! That is the locus of his experience. There are his opportunities for choice. There his character is shaped and his outlook is formed; an outlook that is inevitably projected onto the scene of political affairs and electoral choice. Within a system that has raised him high on tides of taxpayer subvention, public science, and the intervention of the state, the farmer's direct experience in cultivating a plot of land and managing the farm is one of autonomy, self-responsibility, and rugged individualism. From that standpoint, he views the world.

13. George, Henry. *Progress and Poverty.* New York: D. Appleton and Co., 1880.

9 • Policies

Continuing the analysis of elements of the system of technological advance and economic progress, we propose to consider education, the management of science information, the promotion and financing of innovation, and the transformation of industries.

Education

Consider the evolution of our present system of formal education. Its roots are British. In preindustrial Britain, formal education was a monopoly of the aristocracy. Its social role was not to prepare individuals for a function, but for a position in society. Their classical learning set them apart from the common herd; it gave them a class solidarity and a larger perspective on their own place in the continuum of history. The industrial revolution, occurring spontaneously in a world other than that of the educated elite, generated an economy of many small firms that offered the opportunity to acquire the mastery of mechanics and technology through observation and imitation, through apprenticeship and hands-on experience in the family, in the factory, on the farm, and in the shop. Thus, the path of technological learning belonged to another class than the aristocracy; the possession of that technologically critical learning became the basis of bourgeois wealth and power.

As the great corporation replaced the economy of small enterprise, the opportunities to learn by doing on the job, as part of the job, radically diminished. To accommodate the corporate demand for leadership elites, technological training for the varieties of engineers, managers, and research scientists was incorporated into the university curriculum.

This, then, became the normal path of formal education. In the primary and secondary schools, the student is taught the rudiments of literacy and arithmetic; is introduced to history and literature; acquires the beginner's skills in mathematics; is noddingly acquainted with science; and in general, is given a perspective on the modern world and of his and her place in it. At the university, students go more deeply into a selected set of these branches of learning. Only later, at the end of the journey so to speak, they may be trained for some specifically functional role. They exit from the educational system as young officers might, ready to join the ranks of the lieutenants and the captains, eventually destined to map out the strategies and command the troops in the echelons below.

What of those troops on whom these commanders must rely? What of the lower ranks of clerks and technicians, of mechanics and craftsmen, of skilled and unskilled labor on whom the system of technological advance also depends; at a time when there is less opportunity to climb the ladders of skill and status by learning through doing; at a time when the mass migration of skilled and disciplined craftsmen from Europe is no more; at a time when a large and growing underclass, hopeless people, homeless people, lives and breeds in squalor on the public dole, somehow severed from the mainstream, unable to grasp even the lowest rung of the working economy? What is the educational system for them?

This would suggest, as far as technological advance is concerned, that there are two quite different tasks for the American educational system. One is to supply a business elite with the motivation, the skill, the competence to lead and organize the advance of technology. The other is to open the door of opportunity to those outside the system and to the ranks below, to propagate the skills and continuously upgrade the quality of the work force. With regard to both tasks, our present educational system needs to be questioned.

While not entering into the general discourse on educational reform, we have policies to propose: one in relation to the development of business elites, the other in relation to the training and continuous upgrading of the work force; both are important for advancing technology and raising productivity.

Training and Upgrading the Work Force

Whether it does its task well or poorly, our educational system is designed for the selection, recruitment, and development of elites. It has operated under the assumption that the ranks would acquire their skills through apprenticeship or observation on the job, as a part of the job, as might occur on the farm, in the craftsman's shop, or in small enterprise under the control of an individual. In modern, large-scale enterprise, that opportunity is very narrowly constrained. As a consequence, the bulk of American labor has been without the opportunity to acquire complex new skills or to upgrade its competencies either through formal training or through on-the-job learning; a large, wasting underclass is without a way into the system of production.

For possible remedies, we turn again to foreign models. In Japan, the system of formal education is like our own, oriented to the selection and development of elites. But the amount of time and effort devoted to systematic training, designed continuously to upgrade workers from the factory floor, organized by the enterprise, and carried on as part of the normal work load, would amaze the American manager. The private company organizing a worker training program in Japan has this advantage over its counterpart in the United States: Given the stability and attachment of the corporate industrial work force, and the Japanese policy and practice of lifetime employment in the corporate industrial sector, management need hardly fear that investment in worker training will be lost when the trained worker takes a job with a competitor.

The industrial revolution did not occur spontaneously in Germany as it did in England, France, and the United States. It was planned, organized, and imposed by the state. Correspondingly, the state had to organize the education and training not only of a leadership elite, but also of the foot soldiers and petty officers of an industrial work force. Out of this experience emerged their particular educational system, with its two distinctive tracks.[1]

After four years of elementary education, the student, at the age of eleven, enters either the gymnasium or the *hauptschule*. Only 10 percent to 15 percent of the cohort enters the gymnasium, which, like our own system, is geared to the education of elites, and carries the individual toward and through the university. The rest of the cohort enter the *hauptschule*. Of these, about 70 percent follow the basic occupational training course, where classroom work for one day a week is combined with on-the-job training under a two- to three-year contract with an industrial or commercial firm or a craft shop, leading to certification as a skilled worker or qualified office employee. The level of certification determines pay and job opportunity throughout German industry. This apprenticeship system is strictly regulated, and only those certified to do so can supervise and instruct the pupil-workers. Continuing with this combination of classroom instruction and on-the-job training, the worker can climb a ladder of professional licenses to advanced degrees in engineering, and to the upper niches in the corporate hierarchy.

The Japanese approach might be immediately applicable to American industry, but it could reach only those already a part of the industrial work force. To supplement our existing education system with a version of the German *hauptschule*, as an alternative educational track, has the potential for reinvigorating the education for a substantial part of our disaffected youth, and of drawing the children of the underclass into a productive life.

Training Business Elites

In an earlier time, the path to industrial success and leadership, the path of a Carnegie, a Ford, or an Edison, was through the workshop or the factory. Production was the first lesson. Mastery of production was the critical step. Hands-on experience was the teacher. The path to power was conceived in the image of the man who built a better mousetrap, and the world beat a path to his door. That image pointed the way, and that experience shaped the character of the founding leadership. It did not matter that, later, they wore frock coats and dwelled in oak-paneled boardrooms; they understood the organization of production, and they knew that production was the basis of it all.

By the end of World War II, the general character of business life was very different. Where the great industrial corporation held sway, the individual worked as a cog within wheels within wheels of a gigantic machine. It was no longer possible to learn an integral technology or to comprehend the operation of the whole enterprise on the job, as part of the job. It was necessary to abstract and conceptualize observed activities, ordering them into categories of specialization, or integrating them as overarching theory, so they could be taught. Formal education replaced work experience as the critical path to learning. Those who develop technology in the research and development laboratory, recruit and deal with the problems related to company personnel, program computer software, handle company accounts, organize and operate company finance, merchandise and market the company's product, do its business forecasting, handle advertising, promotions, and public relations for the company, deal with taxation and matters of law are university graduates all; formed through processes of formal education.

Where is the fellow who once worked in his shop, and on the side, on his own, built a better mousetrap? He is cranking a screw on the assembly line, light-years away from the locus of industrial power and control. The man who built a better mousetrap is gone from the American mythos. The prevailing, guiding image now is of the entrepreneur, wheeler-dealer, buyer-seller, investment allocator, profit maximizer, and asset manipulator, concerned only with the private payoff and the bottom line, operating in a universe where production is a mere parameter for the feverish manipulation of assets; whose apotheosis is in the takeover artist who knows nothing and cares nothing for the production and technologies of the firms that he controls. For him, the firm, locus of neither his creativity, nor his responsibility, nor his identity, is but a cold object to be traded on the market. With all that comes the precipitous decline of the American system and American technological preeminence.

American business has been chastised by its failures. It is, hopefully, receptive to criticism, and ready for change. To that end, it should look again at the curricula of the schools of business in the United States. Those who earn their M.B.A.s in those schools, as the requisite degree for access to the first rung of the ladder of corporate control, are taught statistics, accounting, finance, marketing, perhaps labor relations, organizational theory, and perhaps operations research. What they are not taught is the organization of production and the management of technology. They begin their careers ignorant of, and unconcerned with, production and technology; ignorant and unconcerned they remain as they climb the ladder toward the apex of control. And, when in control, perforce they will choose a path toward profits other than in the advance of technology, higher productivity, and better production.

That lacuna in their training cries out for curriculum reform.

The Management of Science Information

The product of research and development, whether in corporate research establishments, government research centers, government contractors, or universities, is technologically relevant information. This is an economic resource of enormous importance, and is fundamentally different from any other, for it can be endlessly replicated without cost, and it cannot be exhausted through use. Therefore, the unfettered availability, the free use, and the most extensive and rapid dissemination of technologically relevant information serve the ends of higher productivity and technological advance. The wider its dissemination, the more who are informed, the greater will be its contribution to economic well-being. For that reason, policy should address itself to the many actual barriers to the dissemination and constraints upon the use of the technologically relevant information produced through research and development.

The bulk of public research and development has been for the Pentagon. The military naturally conceives of the world as a field of threat and combat. Its perennial goal is comparative advantage, where what is important is not that we are strong and technologically advanced, but only that, at any level of technology, we are more technologically advanced; hence, stronger than the other. Whatever might be leaked or become known to the other, serving possibly to upgrade the technology of the other, is detrimental. Hence, it is the rule of military intelligence that the fewer who are apprised of the information, the more valuable it will be; which is precisely opposite to the rule of the public benefit. Therefore, the vast volume of Pentagon-sponsored research and development will be kept secret, not only from industry at large, but also from the Pentagon's own researchers, from its own research and development contractors other than those who produced it, even from those with the highest security clearance, unless these have established their "need to know."

The application of this rule of military intelligence does not take into account that withholding the vast body of technologically relevant information produced under military sponsorship (even from other military contractors) suppresses the possible advance of America's own military technology, as well as the technological advance and productivity of industry at large, on which our military prowess also depends. The question is one of balancing the benefit of withholding against the benefit of dissemination. At present, for the officer who makes the judgment as to what to withhold and what to release, nothing is set against the value of eliminating the possibility that disseminated information might possibly be of benefit to the other.

What can be done to achieve some balance in this choice? New classification criteria? An advocacy system to consider the release of categories of information, with experts appointed to argue the pro and con before a judicial board? A periodic review of classified information by a select group from science and business, with the power to appeal classification rulings?

In spite of security classification, great quantities of research and development information produced under public auspices are nevertheless available, from such civilian agencies as the National Aeronautics and Space Administration (NASA), the Department of Health, Education, and Welfare (HEW), the Department of Agriculture, the Department of Energy, and some that escape the classification barriers of the Pentagon. There exists, alas, no apparatus for its systematic dissemination; none to glean the gold from the dross; none to select it for relevance and significance; none to generalize and build on its values for industrial technology. Are there values in that heterogeneous mass worth generalizing and building on? The question cannot be answered, for no assessment has ever been made. It remains a mystery to be resolved, a potential to be explored, a resource yet to be exploited in promoting the advance of technology and the rise of productivity.

There are also important bodies of information produced through corporate research and development, particularly in electronics, chemicals, pharmaceuticals, and synthetics. The private company is normally motivated to withhold all the research and development information it produces as possibly of value to its competitors, except where that information must be revealed because it is embodied in the product offered for sale, in which case, the company may seek to constrain its use through the patent privilege. Or it may offer the information for rent or sale, which would, again, normally require the use of patents.

Consider the case of company X. It is a medium-size pharmaceutical house specializing in psychosomatic medicine. It is currently spending in excess of $70 million annually on research. This research consists of testing the effects of new chemical compounds on animal and human subjects, and organizing the information produced into an instrument for problem solving. During the half century it has been involved in such research, company X has accumulated an enormous store of such information, which it holds secret, available only to its company researchers. Such information is not patentable, but it is the data source from which the company's patented items of psychosomatic medicine derive. It constitutes, in effect, a proprietary sub-science kept secret from all save the company's own researchers.

What is the potential value for the advance of technology at large of this information held now in the private possession of company X; and of the hundreds of other proprietary sub-sciences accumulated elsewhere in the economy? We will not know until the files are examined and an assessment is made; but it can be reasonably hypothesized that the potential value of that information far transcends its contribution to the operation of the specialized companies who possess and use that information; hence that the potential for technological advance would be significantly augmented if that information were made generally and freely available. The catch is this: While making such information fully and freely available would accelerate technological advance, it would also eliminate the profit motivation to invest in research and development. Again, the need for balance. The need is to devise the means of securing a broader dissemination of such information without reducing the corporate motivation to invest in research and development. As one possible approach, we propose the following.

For selected industries, for example, pharmaceuticals or chemicals, a research association would be formed under the sponsorship, and with the participation of, AIM. An AIM team, with established confidentiality, would be empowered to examine and assess the general value of the aforementioned stores of proprietary information. Basing itself on the advice of this team, and acting for the association, AIM would be empowered to use the association's or public funds to procure, at a price, from the company in question such parts of its information store as it considered to be of general value; with this proviso: that information produced within the current year and during the five previous years would remain the exclusive possession of the company that produced it. In effect, this would refund a substantial part of the costs of the earlier research and development expended by the company from whom the research information was purchased, without reducing the value of its current research.

The purchased information, organized as a problem-solving instrument, would become the exclusive possession of the association, available to its dues-paying members. A policy of promoting U.S. competitiveness in the international market could require that only American companies be eligible for membership.

This, while far from a perfect solution, would have these merits: It would broaden the available knowledge base and, hence, augment the creative potential. It would reduce the quasi-monopoly advantage of long-established firms in their prior possession of important bodies of proprietary information, thereby reducing a barrier against new firms entering the industry. By using the revenues obtained through the sale of information produced through its prior research and development to offset current research costs, the costs of ongoing research and development operations would be reduced. On that account, and because the old protective buffer against the incursion of new firms would be gone, new product competition would intensify, and the pressure to invest more in current research and development would increase. If association membership was restricted, the availability of the pooled research and development information would give American companies an advantage vis-à-vis their foreign competition.

Spearheading, Coordinating, and Financing Industrial Development

AIM's primary task would be to rehabilitate laggard and failing industries and to accelerate the advance of American technologies. For that purpose it must initiate, and in tandem with other public agencies, trade unions, and private companies, *target* industrial innovation and development. Targeting is what any firm does in marking out the path and bringing together the elements required to achieve an industrial objective. For the achievement of some objectives, the requisite elements are so disparate, the path to change is so complex as to be beyond the power and competence of any single enterprise. Then targeting requires a coordinating agency such as AIM to engage diverse entities in an integral plan. Thus, for example, the most revolutionary modern technological development in agriculture of the American South was the post–World War II introduction of the mechanical cotton harvester. This was a quite simple innovation that could have arrived half a century earlier if the development of the mechanical cotton harvester had been coordinatable and coordinated with the development of a harvestable cotton plant; that is, one where the cotton did not come into fruition serially to be picked over the course of a season, but at once, so that the whole plant could be torn from the earth and stripped in a single motion by the machine. The mechanical harvester was not developed because it could not be used economically on the cotton as it was then grown in the fields; the harvestable cotton plant was not developed because, in the absence of a mechanical harvester, there was no call for it. Consider another, current dilemma. There are parts of the country where it would be in the national interest, and in the interest of the individual householder as well, to use solar energy for home heating and cooling, provided that mass-produced, low-cost, low-priced equipment was available. Householders do not use solar energy because that equipment is not available, and the equipment is not made available because there is no mass market for it. But the establishment of a mass market for the equipment through the use of regional building codes requiring its installation, coordinated with the targeted development and mass production of low-cost equipment, could resolve the difficulty, *if* there were a coordinating authority able to organize the joint development of the market and the product.

To illustrate the character of targeting and, depending on the concentration and power of private enterprise, the role that AIM, with powers that are both encompassing and detached, might play in the targeting process, consider what was required in establishing a massive new iron and steel industry in post–World War II Japan. The industry had to be located, allocating the steel-making capacity of the new plants in designated ports of call. Numerous suppliers, contractors, and subsidiary producers had to be brought into close proximity with those plants. Inland transportation had to be organized to carry the steel to other manufacturing centers. It was necessary to mobilize and train a large new labor force. Roads, residences, utilities, schools, and so forth were required to accommodate that work force. The world of new and relevant technological developments had to be searched to determine the technologies to be incorporated into the steel-producing complex, through testing and selecting between alternatives and further developing what was currently available. These decisions were risky, innovative, and complex. The Japanese, for example, made the first large-scale use of the oxygen blast furnace and of the continuous casting of steel; they built the largest blast furnaces the world had ever seen, about twice the size of any that existed in the United States. Japan had no iron ore or coal. The price of steel depended on the cost of bringing ore by sea to those designated ports where the industry was concentrated. Partly to meet the need for the ships required for that task, MITI initiated the development of a great new shipbuilding industry, and to minimize the ore-carrying cost, Japan built, in those shipyards, ore carriers of an unprecedented size. These enormous ships needed very deep harbors. So, simultaneously with the building of the ships and the establishing of the steel-making capacity, deep-water harbors (deeper than any that exist in the United States) had to be dredged at the designated Japanese ports of call.

Without assurance that the deep-water harbors would be available, the enormous ships would not have been built; without the capacity to build the ships, the harbors would not have been dredged. Where was the ore to come from? Again, there was a worldwide search, an assessment of alternatives, and negotiations with foreign property owners and foreign governments. Ore deposits in western Australia were selected for exploitation. These were located in a wild part of the Australian subcontinent, without the requisite facilities for their mining, transport, or loading. Simultaneously with the creation of the industry, and the development of the ore carriers and the deep-draft ports in Japan, it was necessary to establish and develop in Australia the ore-mining capacity, the rail transport capacity from mine to port, the on-loading technology for the new carriers, and the deep-draft harbors; all of this as an integral operating system. I have no way of knowing who, among the many participating agencies and companies, is to be credited for doing what in this massive enterprise. It is clear, surely, that it required some initiating, planning, coordinating center.

These, then, are some of the facets of the targeting function:

1. To improve or create the infrastructural frame, for example, in transportation and energy, for the targeted industrial development.

2. To ensure a research and development backup to any targeted industrial development, providing the informational base for planning and subsequently for developing the targeted corporate industrial complex.

3. To ensure the training and mobilization of labor and the availability of finance for each step in the process of industrial transformation.

4. To ensure that all facets of industry are propelled into the future by a research and development center geared into an effective system of technological advance. Such facets of American industry as railroads, urban transit, tunneling and underground construction, housing construction, fisheries, or the cost-reduction side of hospital and medical technology, lack any coherent, effective system for exploring the potentials, developing the technologies, and implementing technological advance.

5. To ensure the existence of integral systems of technological advance including the financial and institutional linkages that carry idea and information into practical application, innovation, and the transformation of industry.

Targeting must be financed, innovation must be financed, growth and development must be financed; the availability and costs of finance is a common denominator of failure and success. We turn now to critique American policy and the American system for financing that which relates to the advance of technology.

Monetary Policy

During President Reagan's second term, the American government, suffering a huge trade deficit, was pressing foreign governments to raise their levels of domestic spending and, in so doing, to increase their imports from the United States. It was reported that Japan was asked to reduce its interest rate from 4 percent down toward 2 percent. At the same time interest rates in the United States were running at from 10 percent to 14 percent; revealing, as by a lightning flash, a handicap on American competitiveness second only to our massive military diversion of resources.

Interest rates will determine the cost of all new financing, including what can be obtained from the sale of common stock. Hence, given the aforementioned difference in interest rates, the costs of financing operations, of expanding operations, of upgrading operations, of establishing new enterprise, or of innovation and the introduction of new technologies will be double, triple, quadruple for American business what they would be for the Japanese. Correspondingly, as interest rates are higher, the feasible range of investment is narrowed, shortened in time, eliminating those high-risk, slowly maturing investments that hold out the possibility of major industrial transformation.

The burden of high interest rates in the American economy is not something that occurs spontaneously, or naturally. It is a burden imposed by the Federal Reserve Board as a matter of monetary policy, allegedly to control inflation. Even in this regard, its effect will be counterproductive inasmuch as it inhibits innovation and the rise of productivity.

How can this heavy burden on the back of American competitiveness be removed? Simply dismantle and cease to rely on monetary policy! Install, in its stead, a system for the management of aggregate spending that does not rely on the manipulation of interest rates, as was spelled out earlier in part 1. But the problem goes deeper, to a malaise at the root of our system for investment finance.

Wall Street

Suppose monetary policy has been dismantled, the Federal Reserve Board concerns itself solely with the viability of the banking system, and interest rates settle at an internationally competitive level. While perfectly able to satisfy the demand for credits in the carrying on of normal business operations, our commercial banks are not designed, intended, or able to fund long-term capital investment. To fund the extension of production, the upgrading of operations, and the development and introduction of new products or technologies, the industrial corporation must either reinvest its profits and/or offer its common or preferred stock or bonds for sale. To satisfy the most vital, socially the most critical, forms of investment, and those that should be based on the deepest knowledge and the most informed judgment of alternatives, the company goes to Wall Street; it has no other option.

Wall Street: How shall we evaluate it as the instrument for the critical and delicate allocation of capital investment?

It emerged from back-street trading, without social design, following its own momentum, its own frenzy, occasionally checked and regulated in the face of scandals and abuses that could no longer be ignored, and disruptions of the economy that could no longer be borne. It operates as a great floating craps game. Its irrational and violent fluctuations produce enormous random changes in the nominal value of national wealth, which, in turn, produce equally random and disruptive changes in consumption and real investment. It opened the way to the buy-outs, takeovers, and conglomerate monstrosities that have carried the Wall Street wheeler-dealer to the heights of industrial power and decision.

If one were free to choose the instrument intended to serve the public interest in the evaluation and allocation of resources between alternative investment opportunities, Wall Street would be the choice of an imbecile. A different instrument is needed that would enable informed and stable financing of industrial development. Again, we take a page from Japan's book of experience, to propose the establishment of a series of development banks, regionally dispersed, and specialized to service different industrial categories.

Development Banks

The development bank would not finance normal business operations. With an initial fund of credit from the central bank, it would operate from a very low basic rate of interest, with charges scaled upward to compensate for risk. The financing of long-range industrial development would be its role and its skill. All loan applications would first be cleared through AIM, and the bank would accommodate AIM's targeting programs.

Development banks, expert in the assessment of production potentials, since their loans must be based on such assessments, would enable more informed allocation of capital investment than Wall Street ever could. The emphasis of a control exercised through the dispersed ownership of shares is inevitably on maximizing current profits, raising current dividends and the market value of shares. The development bank would be indifferent to the scale of current profits. It would necessarily focus, instead, on the capacity of the borrower to meet its interest obligations over the long haul. Consequently, its pressure on its clients would be in the direction of long-range planning, technological development, and solid, stable growth; to the benefit of the operating, resource-employing entity, and of the economy as well.

Note

1. I have tried to follow: Maurice, Marc; Sellier, Francois; and Silvestre, Jean-Jacques. *The Social Foundations of Industrial Power: A Comparison of France and Germany.* Translated by Arthur Goldhammer. Cambridge, MA: The MIT Press, 1986, esp. pp. 28–41.

10 • Crisis

The Heavy Burden of Military
Aggression and Defense

No burden on the economy has been as great, no barrier to the advance of technology and to the raising of productivity in the United States, and the Soviet Union has been comparable, to that imposed by the military expenditure of the two superpowers. Japan and Germany, precisely those countries forbidden the privilege of rearming, led the postwar advance of technology and the rise in productivity and raced to the forefront of productivity and power, while the United States lost a technological preeminence that once had been beyond the reach or aspirations of the rest of the world.

Consider, then, the character and magnitude of the burden borne by the American civil economy for nearly half a century, in the massive deprivation of scientists and research engineers, of skilled and unskilled labor, of managerial and entrepreneurial talents, of machine power and all that goes into expanding, upgrading, and developing industrial capacity and the economic infrastructure. Besides these deprivations, there were distortions of technical education and of corporate industrial research and development as the consequence of the massive military spending.

> The Pentagon's budgets, $2,001 billions, 1946–1981, amounted to 46% of the "reproducible assets" of the U.S. (private and public owned) national wealth: hence about 46% of everything man-made in the United States. From 1981 to 1988 (a mere eight years) the state managers plan fresh military budgets amounting to $2,089 billion—a fund that

equals 48% of the dollar value of the nation's (1975) reproducible assets. . . . When we take into account both the resources used by the military as well as the economic product foregone, then we must appreciate the social cost of the military economy, 1946–1988, as amounting to about twice the "reproducible assets" of the U.S. national wealth.[1]

At issue is not only the enormous diversion of the labor and resources that might otherwise have been used to build roads, bridges, dams, factories, schools, houses, hospitals, railroads and urban transit lines, communication and data processing facilities, machine tools, machines, industrial and medical equipment, and so forth. At least as important is the diversion of a far larger proportion of our science-trained, research-oriented brainpower. In 1962, a not uncharacteristic year, more than 70 percent of all our professional scientists and research engineers were employed directly or indirectly by the military and space agencies. It is a diversion of the high-grade educational talent, not only from industrial laboratories, but also from teaching in schools, colleges, and universities, with consequences for the education of oncoming generations. Finally, it is a diversion from the pool of scientifically knowledgeable, technologically creative entrepreneurship of the sort that produced Silicon Valley on the West Coast and a new flowering of industry in New England. Civilian-oriented industry is thus deprived of its creative potential.[2]

Indifferent to production, operation, or maintenance costs, the Pentagon, in its research grants and procurement practices, focuses on problems of a complexity without analogy in the corporate industrial sector, demanding a capacity for precision that is beyond practical application in civilian industry. Allegedly, Pentagon spending has inculcated an outlook and lured the business community into the acceptance of performance criteria out of kilter with competitive practice and industrial design in the civilian economy. Thus, the U.S Air Force heavily subsidized industrial research in the United States on numerically controlled machine tools. According to Seymour Melman, this so distorted the development of the American technology as to ensure a Japanese sweep of the American civilian industrial market for numerically controlled machine tools.[3]

So, also, according to Herbert Holloman at MIT, those rewards and employment opportunities offered by military procurement have turned engineering education away from the practical and pragmatic needs of industry to serve the esoteric demands of the Pentagon.[4]

No other policy change could hope to reverse the decline of American technology and competitiveness as one that substantially reduced the burden of armaments, with its enormous drain on investable resources and science-trained brainpower. Until yesterday, that seemed impossible. Then I could only plead for a more balanced allocation of resources, since military prowess also depends on a strong civilian industrial economy. (See appendix to this chapter for a discussion.)

The New Vista

What is the reason for the huge defense budget? For an array of weaponry that could destroy the world in half an hour? For the CIA and its apparatus of spying, provocation and sabotage? For NATO? For the American subvention of client states like Pakistan, Israel, El Salvador, and the rest? The only reason, purpose, or justification for all or any of these issues and actions was to defend against the threat to the United States of Communist Russia and Russian communism. Now, suddenly, as in awakening from a dream, for any open-minded observer to see, that threat is gone; if it ever was, it has ceased to be; vanished absolutely.

While, in my view, our responses to Russian communism and to Communist Russia merged into paranoia and fantasy, the threat was real enough as long as communism, an ideology and quasi religion committed to world revolution dominated Soviet policy and held the Soviet Union in tow, with zealots in every country surrendered to its doctrine and obedient to its bidding. Now, communism is finished; dead in the Soviet Union; dead in China; dead in Eastern Europe. Its demise began when Khrushchev exposed the murderous Stalinist regime. Gorbachev only buries the corpse.

The Germanys reunify. The Warsaw Pact is finished. Its former members clamor to join the European Economic Community. Without the cohesive force of communism and the Party, the Russian empire is in a state of disintegration, and Russia strives desperately to survive a period of transition to a still unknown destination. Gorbachev welcomes any offer of mutual disarmament. The total elimination of nuclear arms is in our hands; it is a matter of our choice.

Whatever happens, Communist Russia and Russian communism are no longer a threat, nor is there any prospect that they will become a threat to American security. The justification for our defense budget is gone. Easily, a reduction of 90 percent in our defense spending is in order. That is the first fact.

The Commitment to Balance
the Budget and Reduce Public Debt

For a full decade, the American economy has lived on massive infusions of deficit-based public spending. For a full decade, the sages and the experts, and the pundits, presidents, and politicians of every stripe have railed and warned against the wickedness and dangers of deficit spending, of unbalanced budgets, and of a rapidly mounting national debt. Doubtless, they believed what they preached. The electorate, so inculcated, believes all this as well, and expects its representatives in Congress to act on this belief. Congress is caught between pressure to balance the budget and reduce the public debt, and the real and legitimate needs and demands of the people that Congress remedy a deteriorating infrastructure, a toxic environment, a failing system of education, and so forth, with anathema pronounced on any mention of increased taxation. That dilemma, and the congressional pressure to escape it, is the second fact.

When the first fact sinks into public and congressional awareness, in the full realization that there is no threat to American security from Communist Russia or Russian communism, and therefore, that the justification for military spending has vanished, can it be doubted that Congress will realize and seize upon the opportunity to massively reduce defense expenditure enough to balance the budget, reduce the public debt, and release funds for needed public expenditure without increasing taxation? What happens then?

Crisis

During the 1980s, a brief but sharp reduction of deficit spending produced a major recession. In struggling out of that recession and subsequently, in maintaining a long, steady level of recovery, the American economy was subjected to very large, continuous infusions of deficit-based non-diversionary spending. Hence, it would appear, private consumption and investment propensities being what they are, that heavy and steady infusions of spending that do not divert from, but add to the income-spending stream are needed by the American economy, simply in order to maintain a moderate level of production and employment.

What will happen when Congress, with the options now before it, following its established commitment, does "the right thing" in slashing defense spending, eliminating deficits, balancing the budget, and releasing the enormous resources for so long immobilized and used up in the operation of the military-industrial complex; when those habituated infusions of non-diversionary spending are suddenly withdrawn? Then, the self-renewing level of aggregate spending will accelerate downward. The economy will plunge into a deep depression that spreads rapidly over the rest of the world.

This will not be simply a crisis of underconsumption and underinvestment. It will also have been precipitated and perpetuated by the collapse of the enormous military-industrial complex. That sector will not recover in the normal course of events. No matter what happens to aggregate spending, that sector will be down and out for good. How can we avoid this crisis, or surmount it?

To Cope with the Crisis

To avoid the crisis or, once caught in its toils, to surmount it, the state must be prepared to make heavy new infusions of non-diversionary spending. These need not take the form of deficit finance with the correlated rise in the obligation to pay interest on the public debt. Part 1 of this book made the case against such use of deficit finance, and proposed a painless alternative. It would be a task of the state to prevent or, should it occur, to offset any decline in the level of aggregate demand, and to raise aggregate demand sufficiently above the old norm to draw into full production the resources displaced through the cut in military spending.

One might think of two economies: the normal economy oriented to producing all the goods and services currently consumed by the civil society (economy A), and the military-industrial complex producing the wherewithal of war, generating consumer income, but producing nothing that would satisfy consumer demands (economy B). The income earnings of both economy A and economy B are pumped back as the demand for the product of economy A alone (product A).

With the elimination of military spending, the consumer demands generated through incomes earned in economy B, which hitherto had sustained the production of product A, are eliminated. To avoid the spiraling down of depression, this cut in the demand for product A must be offset by another non-diversionary increase in spending. Suppose that is done, and the old level of aggregate demand sufficient to maintain the production of product A is held constant. There remains another problem, for the resources released from economy B need to be reemployed. To reemploy those resources in an expanded economy A, producing additional product A′, the expenditure norm, via further increments of non-diversionary spending, must increase to include the purchase of products A and A′.

An increase in non-diversionary spending can be induced in the private sector by putting more money in the pockets of consumers through reduced taxes, with no change in the level of public spending; through increased grants and benefits, with no increase in the level of taxation; or, by forcing down the rate of interest, making real investment spending cheaper, hence, more attractive. Or, the required increase in aggregate demand may be achieved by raising the level of non-diversionary public spending. In surmounting this crisis, an increase primarily in public spending must be relied on for the following reasons. Under the threat of economic crisis, with fear and uncertainty rife, it would be difficult to stimulate a significant rise in private investment, no matter how low the rate of interest. A quick and radical increase in per capita consumption in the private sector would also be very hard to achieve, regardless of the cash thrust into consumers' pockets, for consumption habits change slowly; and if the needed expansion could be achieved entirely through a rise in consumer spending, that would increase the danger of inducing expectations of a continuing rate of increase in consumer spending that could not be sustained. Most importantly, very substantial public expenditures will be needed to minimize the waste of talent, to ease the pains of transition in making good use of the resources released from the military-industrial complex.

Thus, for the people and the Congress to recognize and act upon the truth—that there has ceased to be any threat from Communist Russia or Russian communism—and to slash the defense budget accordingly, poses the threat of a major crisis and the need for complex problem solving. This release of the resources held for so long in thrall to the aims of war, contains as well an enormous potential, for the resurgence of our technological preeminence, for the acceleration of technological advance, and for a richer, better life in an era of peace and goodwill.

After World War II

At the end of World War II, there was a massive demobilization and a shift from full-scale war production back to production for civil needs. Yet, no economic crisis occurred. Rather, the world economy slipped quickly into a virtual golden age. Why, then, should there be the threat of crisis now?

During World War II, the tap had been turned off completely on the production for civilian use of automobiles, aircraft, houses, and even whiskey. Food was rationed. The labor shortage and the allocation of critical materials constrained the production of virtually everything else, so that the United States and, even more, the rest of the world were starved for consumer goods.

The war effort had been partly financed through borrowing, but such borrowing was not a roundabout way of enabling an increase in non-diversionary spending intended to raise the level of aggregate demand. Exactly the opposite was the case. Aimed at the ordinary consumer, its purpose was to mop up current purchasing power and to constrain current spending, that is, to divert spending away from civilian consumption to the procurement of military goods and services. It left in the hands of that civilian population, starved for consumer goods, a mass of paper assets convertible into cash, and hence, at the end of the war, into an immediate rise in aggregate demand. The spontaneous rise in consumer demand at the war's end offset the decline in military spending.

The extraordinary and unprecedented GI Bill of Rights subsidized the education, reeducation, and training of returning veterans, facilitating the transition from a war economy to a peacetime economy. In extending to veterans guaranteed low-interest mortgages for the purchase of new housing, it added to the rise in aggregate demand.

West European and Japanese markets, with their bottomless need for consumer goods and capital equipment, were opened to American exports. Those exports were heavily subsidized through the Marshall Plan and other public programs. Arrangements at Bretton Woods made extensive credit available to enable the continuing imports of American production. At home, the installation and extension of social security and other elements of the new welfare state served to raise the level of consumption. All this further offset the decline in military spending.

At that time, there was no sharp demarcation of civil-oriented and military production. Civil industry had converted directly into producing the wherewithal of war, and could easily convert, with a minimum displacement of resources, to producing for the civil market; first, from the production of automobiles to the production of tanks and bombers; then, from tanks and bombers back to the production of automobiles. Even major weapons were converted to civilian use. The planes designed to carry bombs became the workhorses of the civilian airlines. Such conversions are no longer feasible.

The cold war soon began, with the formation of the omnivorous military-industrial complex whose magnitude and power Eisenhower foresaw and warned against. Even by the end of World War II, research and development was relatively peripheral to both the civilian and the military economies. The rare enclaves of scientists and research engineers, as in the Manhattan Project, were quickly and easily absorbed into the universities, with their newly established and government-supported studies on nuclear physics, or into the laboratories of the Atomic Energy Commission, or into the further development of nuclear weaponry under the aegis of the military-industrial complex.

Neither this, nor any equivalent, exists today to ease the transition or to facilitate the deployment of resources released through the closing down of the military-industrial complex.

People and Organizations

Who would be released; what would be affected by the closing down of that establishment? Soldiers, workers, officers, managers, research engineers, and scientists, indeed the whole spectrum of operating personnel, would feel the effects. The destiny not only of people, but also of organizations is at issue. Consider the case of NASA after the triumphant moonshot. The significant product of the $30 billion spent on that great enterprise was not the astronauts walking on the moon, but the great organization that put them there. It was an extraordinary organization, a public organization, efficacious and creative, marked by enthusiasm and dedication, capable of the immense scientific cum technological achievement in opening the path to outer space. It had created a basic new science and technology, radiating the knowledge of these out into the universities and private companies. Jim Webb, the NASA administrator during those, its glory days, pleaded that this organization, unique in the public sector and, indeed, in American experience, be preserved and developed as a multipurpose agency geared to the solution of the high-technology tasks in the public interest. But, under the administration of Richard Nixon (it would have been the same with Ford, Carter, or Reagan), the original NASA was, in fact, destroyed. The moonshot achieved, its funds were cut to the bone. One read of discharge and disorganization, of former physicists running gas stations on the West Coast. A shell of its former self, NASA became a creature of the private contractors with a leadership that came and left by a revolving door to the corporate executive suite. The shuttle disaster, with its passengers burned alive, was the nadir of NASA's decline. At that time, in the Reagan administration, the head of NASA was a borrowed businessman suspended from his office because he was under criminal indictment. The point is this: At issue is not simply the reemployment of persons, but the preservation and re-orientation of successful and effective organizations within the military establishment and peripheral to it.

Options

We envisage and recommend public spending that would not divert from consumption or investment on private or corporate account, that would not incur additional interest-bearing obligations, and that would engage the energies and skills of the disemployed in projects designed to serve the public good.

What kind of projects? What sort of program? We will venture no more than a suggestive layout of options. Because our emphasis is on technological advance and higher productivity, we focus on displacement and redeployment of scientists and research engineers.

The rapid buildup of the military-industrial complex was at the expense of our colleges and universities, depleting their science faculties. The release of scientists and engineers offers an opportunity to rebuild and diversify our system of science education, not only in the universities and colleges, but in our secondary schools as well. The state can support recruitment in two ways: first, in financing an increase in the size of faculties, thereby broadening hiring opportunities; second, in offering educational fellowships to enable the displaced personnel to refurbish, update, and upgrade their knowledge and skills. Those who have been devoting themselves for decades to some special area of research and development that has suddenly become obsolete will need that educational renewal in order to find their way to a teaching niche or to locate elsewhere in the civilian economy. Moreover, if Holloman is right, engineering and science education needs to be reoriented and transformed to satisfy the aims and needs of a dynamic civil economy. It is not unlikely that the guts of that transformation must derive afresh from change-seeking programs targeted by AIM in the corporate industrial sector. What areas might be targeted?

Certainly, energy would be targeted: to discover and develop alternative energy sources to petroleum, natural gas, and nuclear fuel, preferred because they escape or minimize the dangers of depletion, and/or are less costly, and/or are less hazardous than those on which we must now rely. Considerations of costs and safety lead to the study of systems for the transmission of energy. Considerations of public health lead to the search for pollution-free energy sources, and then to other facets of pollution.

Certainly, pollution would be targeted: to develop less costly and more effective technologies for its elimination and control, for the recovery and use of pollutants as useful by-products, for the development of technologies of detoxification, for the more effective and safer disposition of toxic, including nuclear, wastes, and for the development of nontoxic pesticides and systems of pest control. Pollution control, resource conservation, and the protection of the environment, including considerations of global warming and the fate of the ozone layer, all require the continuous monitoring of soil, water, air, and atmosphere, leading to the need to develop a universal system for surveillance and monitoring.

The design and development of a national or transnational grid for the electronic transmission, processing, storage, and retrieval of information would be targeted, with transmission lines carrying information via telephone, cable, earth-orbiting satellite, laser, or microwave, as the situation would require. It would operate as a common carrier with centers for the storage and computer processing of data. It could thus provide the United States with an unprecedented capacity for low-cost, universal surveillance and monitoring of natural phenomena and social event, and information for the continuous formation and implementation of policy. As a system for monitoring natural events and phenomena, it would operate throughout the world, observing through automated means (sensors, cameras, measurement devices) or otherwise, from points on earth or in space, recording, storing, and transmitting observations, interpreting and generalizing on the universe from which the data is drawn through computer programs that operate continuously and autonomously or that are tailored to special problems and transitory phenomena. Thus, through space sensors it would observe, record, and transmit information concerning the condition of the atmospheric layers that enfold the earth. This would be linked to observation and recording of those exudations (wastes, pollutants) from natural catastrophes, industrial chemistry, and atomic radiation, with programs to calculate and chart relationships between those inputs into the atmosphere and the conditions of the biosphere; this would be linked to the worldwide recording, reporting, analysis, and forecasting of temperature and weather, and to the formation and movement of storms, hurricanes, typhoons, tornados, tidal waves, fogs, and floods, with programs continuously exploring climatic and biospheric relationships; that would be linked to the continuous worldwide recording of movements in the earth's crust, its internal geophysical turmoil, soil structures, soil conditions, the nutritional deficiencies of flora as a basis for conservation-planning, for the maintenance or upgrading of soil fertility. It would monitor the location and condition of wildlife and fish populations, the location and migration patterns of locusts and other insects and their predators, the continuous, automated observation and computer-programmed analysis of the chemical composition, levels of pollution, and toxic elements in rivers, lakes, oceans, air currents, soil, and in the food chains in a design to comprehend and control basic ecological systems. Similarly, the grid could be geared to the observation, surveillance, comprehension, and control of economic, demographic, fiscal, epidemiological, medical, and criminal events and phenomena.

If one targeted lacunae in the present spectrum of research and development activity, seeking to spur technological advance in laggard or static areas of the economy, home construction, road building, railroads, urban mass transit, tunneling and underground construction, and the development of lower cost hospital and medical care technologies might be targeted.

Let the reader to whom all this seems fanciful and incomplete bear in mind that our purpose is only to suggest what might be done to put to good use the resources displaced from closing down the military-industrial complex.

Appendix to Chapter 10

In an earlier version of chapter 10, written before our political options were changed by the revolutionary developments in the Soviet Union and Eastern Europe, this was my plea for balance in budgeting military spending.

> There are two alternatives. Real resources can be invested in armaments or in industrial technology. What is invested in one reduces what is available for the other. What is spent for the military reduces the potential for technological advance and for the upgrading of productivity.
>
> The issue is of balance. While no one can know for certain what allocation of resources between the military and industrial technology will achieve the desired level of national security, this much can be said. An optimal level will not be found when no attention is given to, and no account is taken of, the effect of civilian-industrial decline on the military potential, and of the effect of military spending on industrial decline. In fact, public choice has failed to take this dual relationship into account.
>
> More military spending, leaving less for industrial technology, need not spell greater military prowess. It can create military weakness, for the advance of technology and higher productivity in industry spills over into military strength, and the decline of industrial technology spills into military weakness.
>
> During the period between the two world wars, the country that, year after year, invested more resources and more manpower in military preparation than any other was France, and France was overrun in a fortnight. Germany, prevented under treaty from rearming, concentrating its investment into the formation of a powerful industry, in a few years built a military machine that came within a hair's breadth of conquering Europe, Asia, and the world. America's army in the 1920s and early 1930s was hardly more than a garrison force. Until the war was virtually upon us, American military spending was trivial. Then, in a space of four years, the United States emerged as perhaps the greatest military power on earth. The military prowess of the United States derived from, indeed, was based foursquare on an unsurpassed industrial technology. Hence, the inference: to the degree to which military spending reduces (and has reduced) the civilian industrial potential, it reduces (and has reduced) our military potential as well.

Given the extraordinary decline in American industrial technology compared with the rest of the world, and given that the research and development that serves industry is overwhelmed in scale by that which serves the Pentagon, there seems a priori reason to suppose that a voice on the other side, to express concerns that the budgeting of military spending is ultimately detrimental, even to the military prowess of the country, is needed.

One might hope for an agency of counter-advocacy built into the decision process. It would monitor the diversion into the military domain of science-trained brainpower and capital investment and the consequences thereof; it would monitor the possibly distorting effects of military contracting on the business ethos, and the effects of exotic technologies that are the focus of space-military research and development on the university training of engineers and on their consequent capacity to contribute to the advance of civilian-industrial technologies; and it would critique military demands from this point of view. At least there should be some public awareness of the need for balance, and a sensitivity built into congressional deliberations as to the negative effects of military spending on national security.

Notes

1. Melman, Seymour. *Profits without Production*. New York: Alfred Knopf, 1983, pp. 150–51.

2. Solo, Robert A. "Gearing Military R&D to Economic Growth." *Harvard Business Review* (November–December 1962).

3. Melman, Seymour. *Profits without Production*, pp. 4–14.

4. Hollomon, J. Herbert. "America's Technological Dilemma." *Technology Review* (July–August 1971).

PART 4

HOW CAN WE ACHIEVE BALANCED INTERNATIONAL TRADE?

Memorandum

To: Reader
From: Author
Subject: How can we achieve the benefits of stable and balanced international trade?

1. The argument for free international trade starts with the benefits attributed to trade. All such benefits presuppose trade to be balanced in the exchange of goods for goods of equivalent value. International trade, during the decades after World War II, has been in a condition of perpetual imbalance.

2. We propose a reform in the world trading system to achieve balance as the normal condition of international trade, while minimizing the costs, burdens, and disruptions imposed by the trading system on the domestic economies and on the implementation of the domestic economic policies of the trading partners.

3. The rules of the trading system would require that adjustment from a condition of trade imbalance be the task and responsibility of those enjoying trade surpluses rather than, as now, of those suffering trade deficits. It would introduce the systematic procurement of imports purchased on public account for use in the public sector as an optional instrument of adjustment by the countries with a trade surplus.

4. The profoundly destabilizing international flight of cash balances, serving only to change the composition of investment portfolios, would be selectively controlled.

11 • The Benefits of Trade

Policy Options

The argument for free international trade, that canon of ideological liberalism, was contiguous with the emergence of modern economics. It was the call of Adam Smith's *Wealth of Nations*. It was the link between the theories of Adam Smith and David Ricardo. During the centuries since Smith and Ricardo, it has been an argument that has frequently triumphed, but never entirely conquered. It remains today, as it has for two centuries, contesting the policy ground with two other policy options. One of these we might term the *mercantilist*; the other, the *autarkic*.

The liberal argument holds that the policy objective should be to promote and facilitate trade freely entered into by buyers and sellers among all the nations. The mercantilist argument holds that the policy objective should be to create a favorable balance of trade, that is, a surplus in the export of goods and services matched by an influx of money. The autarkic argument holds that international trade should be limited or eliminated if and inasmuch as it introduces an uncontrolled variable into the internal operation of the economy, and thereby interferes with the domestic objectives of economic policy. The departure of nation after nation from a policy of free trade, and the eventual dissolution of the gold standard during the depression years of the 1920s and 1930s, followed the autarkic option.

This chapter will contrast the liberal and mercantilist arguments. Autarky will be considered in part 5.

The Preference for Mercantilism

The mercantilism confronted by Adam Smith in his *Wealth of Nations* was the reasoned doctrine of a statecraft that had as its objective the building of a nation. When the king was but the first among equals, and his barons were autonomous, the power of the nation and the possibility of a national law depended on the king's own power, which, in turn, depended on the king's own wealth. It was through the royal command over the influx of money produced through an export surplus that the coffers of the crown could be filled with gold and specie. Thus, the crown acquired the wherewithal to hire and equip the armies and navies needed to fight its enemies abroad and to subdue the barons at home. It was Adam Smith's message that the barons had already been subdued. Their autonomy was gone. The power of the nation depended no longer on the gold in the coffers of the crown, but on the productivity and the taxable wealth of the whole people.

Although this initial justification for mercantilist trade policy is long obsolete and has almost vanished from memory, the political commitment to a mercantilist policy remains very strong, rooted in the perception of individual self-interest. Capital and labor are self-interested, not in exchanging goods for goods, but in expanding the export of their product while containing or reducing competitive imports. For labor, more exports mean more jobs, more demand for the energy and skills of the worker, and higher pay. For capital, exports signal greater sales, production, and profits. Conversely, imports are seen as a threat to domestic employment, production, and profits. From this perspective, exports are beneficial, and imports are harmful; hence, the objective of policy should be to promote as large a trade surplus as possible.

Whatever the quality of its logic, this mercantilist motivation is omnipresent, although it may come disguised in liberal clothing. Thus, at the end of World War II, the American government became the great advocate of free trade. That was a time when American technology was so far in advance of anyone else's that trade, free of constraint from the exporter or the importer, would guarantee an American trade surplus. To capital and organized labor in the United States, free trade meant an American trade surplus. That mercantilist objective brought organized labor and the great industrial corporations into the game, together with ideological liberals, under the banner of free trade.

This preference for mercantilism can be discounted, in part, as based on a fallacious perception, deriving from the discrepancy between a public choice that proceeds from an evaluation of the interest of the whole, and one that reflects the sum of individual interests. If the individual exporter was not paid for the goods he sold abroad, he would soon be up in arms and outrage. But, as the system operates, the exporter is not concerned that the value of goods exported is not balanced against the value of goods imported, so that society and the economy as a whole are not receiving value for value in the export transaction, but rather are giving up something for which nothing is received in return. No matter that the society is being shortchanged, each particular exporting organization is paid in full. It is enriched. The goods and services it exports are, under condition of trade surplus, paid for, not with goods from abroad, but with goods and services produced at home. Nor, since domestic consumers have no knowledge of them, can they have a reason to complain about the benefits that would have been theirs if international trade accounts were kept in balance.

The Economic Value
of a Favorable Balance of Trade

The persistence of mercantilist policy has another, pragmatic justification. Thomas Malthus noted long ago that a favorable balance of trade and the consequent influx of money from abroad offered more than benefits to exporters and those who produced for export. It also gave a lift to the whole economy. It brought general prosperity and a higher level of employment. To that end, the systematic pursuit of a favorable trade balance became an objective of statecraft, and an important element in the colonialism or imperialism of the nineteenth century.

It is a zero-sum game. An export surplus here must be matched by an export deficit there; the favorable balance is somewhere equated to an unfavorable balance. If the export surplus brings prosperity to one nation, through the converse operation of the same mechanism, the export deficit must have the opposite effect on a trading partner, draining funds from its economy, diverting spending from its domestic market. The threat of depression was deepened by an unfavorable balance of trade. The pursuit of export surplus is ultimately a beggar-thy-neighbor policy. It invites retaliation. It generates conflict and tension among the nations. Only a condition of trade balance, without trade deficit and trade surplus, with exports matched by imports, weaves the nations together with ties of mutual benefit and interdependence, and creates the basis for international stability.

Still, this beggar-thy-neighbor tactic has been capitalism's classic mode of combating unemployment. If one takes as given an irremediable condition of underemployment, then, regardless of its dangers, some would consider it properly in the national interest to pursue ruthlessly a favorable trade balance. Given an irremediable condition of underemployment, it would be better to waste resources as exports for which nothing is received in return; better, indeed, to produce and then dump the product of unemployed labor into the sea, rather than allow the human resource to waste in enforced idleness. With an irremediable condition of underemployment, a policy and practice that promotes and perpetuates trade surplus in order to provide "jobs, jobs, jobs," in the short run at least, has its pragmatic value. But one need not, and we do not, accept the condition of underemployment as given or irremediable.

Keynes made clear that the reason a trade surplus can bring prosperity to the exporting country's economy is because the net inflow of funds from abroad raises, by some multiple of itself, the level of aggregate spending. But there are other ways to raise the level of aggregate spending than through a trade surplus. (The theory was explained earlier in chapters 1 through 3.) Keynes would have maintained that the rational domestic management of aggregate spending can ensure a full employment without throwing away resources via an export surplus. We reserve the question of whether international trade itself interferes with and prevents the effective domestic management of aggregate expenditure for a discussion of the autarky option in part 5.

The condition of export surplus must be transitory, discontinuous, destabilizing, and uncertain. Those who through trade deficits lose their gold and foreign exchange must eventually stop importing; then, trade dwindles and dies, and the positive benefits of true exchange, good for good, are lost.

The Benefits of Trade

What are the benefits of true exchange? The argument for a regime of free international trade projects a metaphor of an exchange between individuals. No rational individual would freely enter into an exchange unless it was in the interest of that individual to do so. Hence, the exchange must be to the advantage of all trading partners, or else they would not have entered into it. Therefore, trade between rational individuals must benefit all who engage in it. By analogy, the same must be true for trade between nations.

In fact, individuals do not barter good for good. They sell for money; they buy with money. Economics makes the case that, although operating through the money nexus, given balanced trade in a properly functioning market, each nation, like each individual, freely entering into an act of exchange, will give up that which it values less for that which it values more, to the benefit of all parties to the exchange.

But, the important benefit is not in a more desirable distribution of a given set of goods between individuals or between nations. Trade would enable, and free trade with competition would require, that each of the trading partners specialize in the production and export of that in which it is relatively the most efficient. This would result in the optimal use of the world's resources, and hence, in a larger gross output to be divided among the trading nations.

Balance

We underscore the following:

1. The mercantilist arguments assume and require the assumption of imbalanced exchange. The objective of mercantilist policy is to create and maintain a condition of trade imbalance. The rational objective of a liberal free trade policy is to enable and maintain a condition of balanced exchange.

2. The argument for free trade holds that trade, in the sense of the *balanced* exchange of goods for goods where the value of exports is equal to the value of imports, is inherently desirable.

3. The rationale of free trade requires the assumption that international trade is balanced. Without a balanced exchange of goods for goods of equivalent value, none of the alleged benefits would hold.

12 • The Continuum of Imbalance

The Trading System

To evaluate the international trading system, we propose the following criteria:

1. The benefits of trade require balanced exchange, where the value of exports is equal to the value of imports for all parties to the exchange. A world trading system should be judged for its capacity to maintain a condition of balance, goods for goods, value for value, among the trading partners.

2. The system also should be judged as to whether its operation hinders and deters or, conversely, facilitates and promotes exchange by minimizing uncertainty and stabilizing expectations in relation to international trade relationships.

3. A final criterion would involve an analysis of the costs and burdens the system's operation imposes on the domestic economies of the countries engaged in trade.

Evolution of the World Trading System

Great Britain dominated both thought and practice in the organization of international trade throughout the nineteenth century. Under its imperial aegis, a set of rules evolved for self-regulation of international exchange by the trading nations. These rules were accepted by statesmen almost as a code of national honor, by bankers as honest practice, and by economists as rational policy.

Under these rules, the monetary authority (treasury or central bank) of each nation undertook to maintain the value of its currency in fixed relation to the other currencies of the world through the open offer to repurchase its currency from the foreigner for gold at a fixed rate of exchange. Hence, with gold as the common denominator, the value of each currency was fixed in relation to every other. Each nation's monetary authority, monopolizing the exchange of currencies, acquired its fund of gold and foreign currencies from payments received by its nationals for their exports, and in exchange for receipt of the home currency, the monetary authority paid out gold or foreign currencies to cover the cost of whatever its nationals imported from abroad.

When the expenditures on a nation's imports were greater than the market value of its exports, the outflow of gold and foreign currency would exceed its inflow, and the monetary authority's reserves of foreign exchange would be depleted. To protect those reserves and hence, the value of its currency, that movement of funds must be reversed. To do this, the monetary authority raised interest rates and tightened credit domestically. The high interest rates, it was supposed, would attract funds from abroad to purchase the securities on which the higher rates of interest were being paid. That inflow would, at least in the short run, replenish the reserves of foreign exchange. In the longer run, it was supposed that tighter money at home would reduce domestic incomes and spending, and deflate domestic prices in relation to prices abroad. With their income reduced, consumers would spend less on both domestic and imported products. They would also shift a proportion of their purchases from the imported to the now lower-priced domestic product. On both counts, spending on imports would decrease. Relatively lower prices of the domestic products would stimulate an increase in their export. More exports and fewer imports would eliminate the trade deficit and bring trade back to a condition of balance.

If that did not work, if the domestic price level refused to sink downward, if, in spite of everything, the value of imports continued to exceed that of exports, and the funds of foreign exchange continued to dwindle, then the state would devalue its currency, making its own money cheaper in relation to gold and, hence, in relation to foreign currencies. The unusual step of devaluation was resisted by the international business community, because it introduced debilitating instability and uncertainties into their contractual relationships; by statesmen, because devaluation was taken to be a sign of national weakness; by bankers, who feared that foreigners, with no more confidence in the integrity of the national currency, would bank their funds and entrust their savings to financial institutions elsewhere.[1]

This was the classical system of international trade. By its firmly established exchange ratios, it stabilized the parameters of international exchange, and in that way, facilitated the extension of international trade and investment. On the other hand, in addition to the not inconsiderable real costs of acquiring the requisite gold reserve, it placed the full burden for the adjustment of trade imbalance on the domestic economies of the trading nations. Through the instrumented flux of interest rates, manipulating domestic incomes and price levels as the means of achieving a trade balance, instability and uncertainty were shifted from the international to the domestic economy.

Into the twentieth century, in economies dominated by a corporate industrial sector, there occurred a fundamental change in the character of economic instability. Deflationary measures undertaken to equilibrate trade did not so much reduce price levels as create mass unemployment. The advent of the Great Depression shifted the focus of public concern away from preserving stable parameters for international trade to the amelioration of domestic crisis. What had been an almost sacred commitment to fixed and stable international currency exchange ratios disappeared. One country after another broke from the obligation to maintain those ratios, broke from the gold standard, freeing itself to use all its monetary and fiscal powers to bring about the reemployment of labor, and to raise the levels of industrial production at home.

In the full flush of post–World War II prosperity, the focus of policy changed again. Especially, the American government sought to promote the extension of international trade through the coordinated elimination of trade barriers, and by reestablishing stable exchange parameters for international trade and contract. The commitment to fixed exchange ratios was revived, except that the American dollar was now so strong, so much in demand, that it was used by central banks in lieu of gold. Dollar reserves were accumulated, and the dollar became the standard to which all the world's currencies were pegged. At Bretton Woods, an international bank was established and authorized to make loans to member countries out of the reserves of currencies contributed by the member countries to the bank, thereby allowing the nations greater leeway in offsetting trade imbalances.

The foundation of the new exchange system was the strength of the

American dollar; the system collapsed when its foundation crumbled. American trade surpluses had turned into trade deficits. In the 1960s, a series of currency revaluations began, lowering the value of the dollar in relation to other currencies. Finally, the dollar-based system, with monetary authorities committed to maintaining currencies in fixed ratios to each other, was replaced with a nonsystem of floating exchange rates.

With no governmental intervention, free from any deliberated policy, all relationships between currencies were to be left to the free market in New York, London, Zurich, Tokyo, and Hong Kong. Currency values, it was supposed, would find their natural level, and trade would be stabilized at the point where currency values found their equilibrium.

Floating exchange rates did not bring the actual exchange of goods and services into a stable equilibrium. Trade was not balanced; it remained in a state of unceasing and increasing imbalance. American trade deficits increased year after year.

Exchange ratios were endlessly destabilized, changing swiftly and unpredictably, sometimes requiring ad hoc multinational interventions. More than ever, exchange rates were distanced from comparative, country-to-country procurement values. Exchange rates found their equilibrium in the speculative trading, back and forth, of the huge stocks of diverse currencies and of gold in private hands, rather than in comparative national productivities. The magnitude of those stocks was a matter of historical happenstance. The demand for them shifted with speculative fears and fevers beyond logical accounting. The new preeminence of the international corporation as a bridge in the transnational flow of goods and services served, perhaps, as a means of surmounting the instabilities and uncertainties thus inserted into the terms of trade.

The new instabilities of exchange were not offset by greater stability and control at home. With the post–World War II extension of international trading, each national economy had become more vulnerable to the economic condition of its trading partners. Severe recession in the United States in 1980 brought Western Europe down from the high plateau of prosperity and growth it had enjoyed for decades. This was as a consequence of (1) the reduced American market for European imports and (2) an anti-inflationary tight-money policy raising interest rates in the United States, with Europeans forced to follow suit in order to defend their disappearing cash balances.

Evaluating the Trade System

Earlier, we proposed three criteria for the evaluation of an international trading system: (1) that its operation facilitates and promotes the organization and extension of international trade through minimizing uncertainty and stabilizing expectations; (2) that it minimizes the costs and burdens of adjustment imposed on the domestic economies of the countries engaged in trade; and (3) that it maintains a condition of trade balance, goods for goods, value for value, as the norm among the trading partners.

The world trading systems have not met these criteria. The most total and spectacular failure has been under the current regime of free-floating exchange rates. Under the current system, exchange rate ratios are randomly unstable, subject to unbounded speculative swings; uncertainty is pervasive. This instability in the international economy has not been offset by any gain of autonomy and control in the domestic economies of the trading partners. Each is constrained by the actions of the others. Thus, a twist of American policy dragged Western Europe into the slough of sustained recession. The system has not produced a general condition of trade balance. On the contrary, the post–World War II decades have been a continuum of imbalances.

The Continuum of Imbalance

The benefits claimed for trade vanish, and the arguments for free trade are meaningless, in the face of experienced conditions of great trade surpluses here and enormous trade deficits there, in a shifting continuum of imbalance. It is a record of failure that raises the question as to whether, under the observed conditions of perpetual trade imbalance, there are any gains from trade.

The pain of those who suffer deficits is clear enough: an unwonted debt that can become unpayable, mass unemployment, and ravaged industries, suffocated under a flood of imports. Even if the deficits are transitory, the delicate and complex social and economic relations that make for a viable industry may be irreparably destroyed.

What of the joy of those who "enjoy" a trade surplus? Exports in excess of imports are in no sense a benefit of exchange. The size of the export surplus measures, rather, the loss of real resources that might otherwise have provided more of the good things in life to the people of the exporting nation. It is a measure of waste of the goods and services sent abroad (to the detriment of those who suffer trade deficits), for which nothing is received in return.

Waste and distortion on both sides: For those who suffer the deficits there are the wastes of industrial devastation and unemployment; those who enjoy surpluses are throwing away what could have been used to satisfy their people's needs.

The free trader cannot deny the swings of deficit and surplus in a perpetuity of imbalance. He might argue that, eventually, in the long run, old deficits will be offset by new surpluses, and old surpluses will be offset by new deficits. I know of no historical evidence to support that supposition. Even if it is true, it is no answer. It means, merely, that the trading nations change places in the character of the wastes and distortions that they suffer. Waste and distortion goes on apace. The discontinuities take their toll. True trade, the equilibrium state of mutually advantageous exchange, escapes our grasp.

Question

This, then, is our question: Can we devise a trading system that will meet the three criteria: that it minimize the costs and the burdens of adjustment imposed on the domestic economies of those engaged in trade; that it promote and facilitate the organization and extension of trade by minimizing uncertainties and stabilizing expectations; and that it ensure a general condition of trade balance? Chapter 13 offers a positive answer to that question.

Note

1. As it turns out, a lowering of the domestic price level of the country in deficit, no matter how achieved, need not turn the balance of trade. The drop in the selling price may more than offset the increase in physical quantities sold, so that the value of exports goes down rather than up, that is, it is a matter of the elasticity of the demand and supply functions.

13 • Finding Balance

If society could achieve balance as the normal condition of international trade, then the classical demonstrations of the gains from trade would regain their force. Inasmuch as trade is balanced, so that neither deficits nor surpluses are accumulating, and there is no need to resort to measures that impose disruption and distortion on the domestic economy in order to correct a state of imbalance, then the instabilities, discontinuities, and uncertainties specific to a system of international trade would be eliminated.

We will argue that international trade can be balanced. The swings of surplus and deficit can be avoided. Exchange rates can be stabilized. This can be done without adverse effects on the domestic economies of the trading partners, through the following simple and feasible changes in the rules of the international trading game.

New Rules for International Trade

1. In a return to earlier and traditional practice, the monetary authorities (treasury or central bank) of each of the trading nations would exercise control over currency exchange within their sovereign domain. All foreign exchange transactions would be conducted only through the monetary authority or its agents. Exporters would be free to use their foreign earnings to purchase the domestic currency from the monetary authority, and importers would be free to use the domestic currency to purchase foreign currencies from the monetary authority at a fixed rate of exchange. An influx of foreign currencies in excess of their outflow (via a favorable trade balance) might be retained and accumulated as a reserve by the monetary authority.

2. Through a consortium of the trading nations (the institutional base is available for coordinated action by such a consortium), rates of exchange would be set by reference to comparative price levels and factor costs in the trading nations; so that, for example, a dollar could purchase as much in Bonn as it would in New York, and the yen, as much in London as in Tokyo. As in earlier and traditional practice, the monetary authorities of all the trading nations would pay out foreign currencies in return for their own currency at those fixed rates.

3. Periodically, or in response to a petition from its members, the international trade consortium would reexamine the whole matrix of currency exchange rates, adjusting them with reference to changes in relative factor costs and output prices as appropriate.

4. By prior agreement, the monetary authorities of each of the trading nations would be allowed to accumulate a reserve of foreign currencies up to a predetermined limit, constituting a substantial margin of safety. No trading nation would be allowed, again, by prior agreement and under international pressure and sanction, to accumulate foreign currency reserves beyond that limit.

When, as a consequence of the trade surplus, the influx of currency from abroad exceeds the sanctioned reserve limit, it would be the obligation of the government of the country with the surplus to reverse the flow.

This represents a sharp departure from, indeed, it is a reversal of traditional practice, for it puts the burden of adjustment on the recipient of the trade surplus, rather than, as hitherto, on those incurring deficits.

It would be far easier for the actor, and less disruptive for the world economy, that the adjustment be made through the disposition of a surplus rather than through making up a deficit.

Reversing the Trade Flow

Aside from petitioning the consortium to review and revise exchange rate relationships, the recipient of the favorable balance of trade would have the following options in eliminating its trade surplus.

1. It could accelerate the growth of its own GNP by raising the level of aggregate spending in Keynesian fashion, with more spent for both domestic and imported goods, causing imports to increase. If more spending raised the price of the factors of production, hence, of

home-produced goods, that would reduce exports. Through increased imports and reduced exports, the trade flow might be reversed and brought into balance. The obvious problem with this solution is that it constitutes a very crude instrument of adjustment, having effects far beyond international trade, and might precipitate an unwonted inflation.

2. It could correct the trade flow by taxing selected exports and/or subsidizing selected imports (a reversal of current practice). This would minimize the effects of adjustment on the domestic economy, and enable preferred imports to be protected. In correcting a trade surplus, it would be to its interest to remove barriers and informal constraints on imports.

3. It could use the foreign exchange surplus accumulated in the vaults of the monetary authority to procure and import goods and services on public account for use in the public sector, or for private consumption under public aegis, thereby more fully satisfying collective needs and social goals, without in any way disturbing the industrial and commercial relationships of the domestic economy.

Public procurement of goods and services to be used in the public sector would be the most certain, the most expeditious, and the least disruptive way of bringing trade flows into balance. It is the neglected wild card in the control of international trade flows and in the settlement of international debt.

The Systemic Use of Public Procurement

Regardless of free market pretensions, all modern states have a large and vital public sector, in health, education, defense, and the key components of the infrastructure, where spending is not competitive with, but supports and complements, private transactions in the market economy.

Suppose, as the consequence of trade surplus, there is immobilized in the vaults of a country's central bank a fund of foreign currencies in excess of the reserves allowed under the international agreement. The government could spend those reserves to import goods and services to help satisfy the goals and needs of the public sector. This sheer addition to the established level of public spending would yield public sector benefits with no increase in debt or taxation, and with no inflationary pressure on the domestic economy. The gap in trade would be filled by imports on public account. Trade could thus be brought into balance with harm to none and benefit to many. Aside from the use of this technique in balancing international trade accounts, it has a role to play in the settlement of any debt arising from intergovernmental transactions. A rare but important instance of its use was in Senator Fulbright's famous plan enacted into law at the end of World War II. Under this plan, the United States turned over to its Allies the bases and properties it had established in Europe during the war, accepting in payment not gold or dollars but the local currency of the country taking possession of that property. Those funds were used by the American government to pay for the education of American students and for research by American scientists and scholars in Europe's great universities. This turned out to be one of the happiest events of the postwar era, significantly raising the level of American science and art.

After World War I, it is said, Lloyd George, the British prime minister, advocated a "hard" peace, demanding heavy reparations from Germany, until his economic advisers, John Maynard Keynes among them, gave him a lesson in neoclassical economics; pointing out that the Germans could only obtain the funds required to make settlement by dumping German goods, especially coal from the Ruhr, on British and world markets (selling massively and cheaply and buying nothing in return). This would disrupt and even destroy viable business organizations and established trade relations, as, for example, in the coal mining industry in Wales. Those trade relations were but the outward manifestation of an underlying balance of ongoing processes, of complex and delicately integrated networks of skills, commitments, and expectations created through generations. Once disrupted, they might never be repaired.

The prime minister considered the effect the dumping of German coal would have on his own poverty-ridden Welsh mining constituencies, and he changed his mind. He advocated a "soft" peace, with reparations eliminated entirely. This was a sensible calculation of British interests *if* reparations were to be made by Germany paying in pounds sterling earned through market sales in the private sector. Then, the transitory availability of cheap German imports would not have been worth the suffering among producers and the disruption of established market relationships that it would create. But the reparations could have been transacted in ways other than private sales in the market sector. There could have been an arrangement between national states to meet collective needs in the British public sector, without affecting market relationships. Through reparations paid in German currency, Lloyd George might have imported German equipment and engineering services to make the Welsh coal mines safe and productive, possibly avoiding the years of disaster for British coal that lay ahead.

Remember the Marshall Plan? Following World War II, moved by compassion and motivated by anticommunism, Americans financed the export of billions of dollars worth of goods and services to refurbish the economies of old friend and old foe alike. No repayment was asked for. Why not? The American government was swayed by the same argument that had convinced Lloyd George.

Europe and Japan, it was alleged, could accumulate the dollar surplus required to repay such an enormous debt only by excluding American exports and/or by flooding American and world markets with goods sold at desperation prices, to the detriment of American industry. The United States would then be under political pressure to retaliate with tariffs and quotas against Japanese and European imports. As a result, world trade would spiral downward. Because the Japanese and Europeans would then be unable to sell enough to acquire the dollars needed to repay their debt, repayment would be kept forever out of reach. The American government determined that a giveaway was better than a loan with such consequences.

That argument, although incongruous now in the light of American trade deficits, made sense at the time, assuming that trade imbalance could be adjusted only through market transactions in the private sector. If procurement under governmental aegis for consumption in the public sector had been recognized as an alternative mode of repayment, the Marshall Plan need not have been a giveaway. Repayment could have served either to offset deficits, should they occur in the course of private trade (as has been the case), or alternatively, to procure and consume goods and services on public account outside the web of market transactions.

The Transformed Trading System

A world trading system that put the responsibility for overcoming trade imbalance on the recipients of trade surplus rather than on those who suffer deficits, and that systematically uses the reserves accumulated through a favorable balance of trade for the public procurement of imports for public sector consumption, at least as a transitory means of balancing accounts, would achieve a continuing condition of trade balance, with international trade encouraged through the stabilization of the parameters of exchange, and with minimal adverse effects on the domestic economies of the trading nations. The system, however, would not be without its problems. If, for example, the U.S. monetary authority spent a part of the reserves accumulated from a trade surplus to procure imports on public account, it would preserve a situation where it would be paying out more dollars to the importers in the private sector than it would be receiving dollars from the exporters in the private sector. This would create a net addition to the stream of domestic spending, that need not be in accord with the objectives of expenditure management.

14 • The International Flight of Cash Balances

International Investment versus Portfolio Shifts

In order to enable multiparty trade, nations or individuals do not barter goods for goods. They sell for money. They buy with money. Hence, to the flow of goods there is a crossflow of finance. Money moves to purchase imports and counterwise to pay for exports. Other than as an instrument of trade, there is the financial flow of investment. Forms of international investment, serving no socially useful purpose, can disrupt the implementation of domestic policy, thwart trade balance, and by their movement, drag nations into recession or inflation as the consequence of policies other than their own. This chapter will diagnose this pathology and will propose a cure.

We must differentiate between (1) "real" investment that finances the establishment of enterprise or develops or extends a mercantile or industrial operation; and (2) investment that adds nothing to the productive capabilities of the economy, but, through the purchase of paper assets like corporate and government bonds and securities, has an effect on ownership portfolios.

"Real" international investment to finance the establishment of an enterprise or to develop or extend mercantile or industrial operations, will be discussed in part 5 of this book. In this chapter our concern is with investment of the second sort, the international flight of cash balances that serves only to shift portfolio holdings, e.g., a bank in Hamburg, West Germany, sells its German bonds for marks, uses these to buy dollars in Zurich, uses the dollars to buy government bonds in the United States which pay a higher rate of interest than do the German bonds, thereby rendering its portfolio more lucrative than before. The problems of this form of cash flow must be understood in the interaction of the money market, international trade, and the conduct of domestic economic policy.

The Money Market and International Trade

The large and complex international market for the different national currencies has become of preeminent importance under a regime of free-floating exchange. The great stocks of national currencies in private, corporate, and public possession are traded back and forth in anticipation of future values, for the purpose of hedging, or to satisfy operating needs: yen to buy dollars, dollars to buy francs, francs to buy pesos, pounds sterling to buy marks, and so forth. The outcome of such trading determines the relative price of currencies, that is, the rates of exchange.

The effect of trade surplus or deficit on the relative values of currencies can be overridden by countervailing portfolio demands or by speculative trading of vast, already existing currency stocks.

The Money Market, International
Trade, and Domestic Policy

With this as background, we can demonstrate the dangers implicit in the transnational flight of speculative cash balances, taking a concrete instance of West European and United States policies.

During the Carter and Reagan administrations, at a time when the country was experiencing large and continuing trade deficits, the American government massively increased its debt. It did this for two reasons. First, the U.S. Treasury borrowed to cover the difference between public spending and public revenues at the conjunction of a radical increase in military expenditures and the political commitment to reduce taxation. Second, in its anti-inflationary monetary policy, the Federal Reserve Board sold government bonds in order to take money out of the commercial banking system, thereby shrinking the cash reserve available to the banks and narrowing the limits of their power to lend, thus tightening credit and forcing up the rate of interest. In this instance the Federal Reserve Board drove interest rates to heights not experienced in more than half a century.

To judge the paradoxical events that followed, keep in mind that in this case deficit finance was intended not to add more dollars to the income-expenditure stream but, in order to act against inflation, deficit finance was intended to take dollars out of the income-expenditure stream. While the Federal Reserve Board was pulling dollars out of the banking system in pursuit of its policy, the high interest rates, which were the result of that policy, were pulling dollars from abroad back into the banking system. The more dollars that came back into the banking system, the more the Federal Reserve Board was obliged by its policy to sell government securities, increasing the public debt in order to draw those dollars from abroad out of the banking system.

Suppose there is a $500 million cash reserve in our commercial banking system. In order to constrain credit so that the rate of interest will rise to X percent, the monetary authority sells $100 million in government bonds and withdraws the $100 million received for those bonds from the banking system. The rate of interest goes up to X percent. The Federal Reserve Board has achieved its goal, and in doing so has increased the public debt by $100 million. This very high rate of interest draws dollars from abroad into the American economy, thence into its banking system. As long as this inflow of speculative cash balances from abroad to purchase those high-interest-bearing securities continues, the Federal Reserve Board must keep selling more government bonds, cumulatively increasing the public debt, in order to withdraw the inflowing dollars from the banking system, for no purpose other than to prevent an increase in the cash reserves of commercial banks, thereby maintaining its anti-inflationary rate of interest.

This transaction results in no real investment in the American economy, no installation of industrial capacity, no establishment or extension of productive operations. It has simply shifted ownership claims into the hands of foreign individuals and institutions for which the American economy received nothing in return. It did not, as is often alleged, finance the increase in the public debt. On the contrary, it was the influx of funds from abroad that caused the increase in the public debt. Without that influx there would not have been that increase. It disrupted domestic policy in the United States in frustrating the efforts of the Federal Reserve Board to hold down the cash reserves of the commercial banks to a predetermined level. And the consequent increase in the foreign debt helped to turn this once great creditor into the largest debtor nation in the world.

The flight of international cash balances in the direction of super-high interest rates in the United States had other consequences. The holders of cash balances abroad in pesos or marks or francs or pounds or lira, wanting to shift their portfolio holdings into more U.S. securities, used their currency to buy dollars in the money market. That raised the value of the dollar relative to other currencies at a time when huge and accumulating American trade deficits should have had the opposite effect. To consumers in other countries, the increase in the value of the dollar meant an increase in the cost of American goods and services. Therefore they bought fewer American goods and services; imports from the United States declined. Conversely, for Americans, the cost of foreign goods and services declined and hence imports from abroad increased. More imports, fewer exports meant a continuing trade deficit. The trade deficit feeds dollar surplus into the international money market. One might expect that the increase in the supply of dollars would reduce the value of the dollar and re-equilibrate trade, but with the lure of high-yielding American securities, foreign individuals and institutions use their yen, francs, pesos, marks, pounds, and lira to purchase dollars with which to buy those high-interest-bearing securities in the United States. Their purchases keep the dollar overvalued, perpetuating imbalance, trade deficit, and the outflow of dollars into the international money market. The dollars, lost in the trade deficit, come back into the American banking system through the foreigners' purchase of high-yield U.S. securities. The increase in their cash reserves raises the lending potential of the American commercial banks. To exploit that potential, they compete for new borrowers. This competition forces down the rate of interest, annulling the anti-inflation strategy of the Federal Reserve Board. To protect its policy, the Federal Reserve Board sells more government bonds to sop up the dollar influx, which further increases the size of the national debt and its interest obligation.

The Federal Reserve Board sells U.S. bonds to remove dollars from the American banking system. Dollar balances from abroad return to purchase those bonds. This flight of cash balances to buy the high-interest-bearing debt, preserves an overvalued dollar, thwarts trade balance, and perpetuates American trade deficits. The deficit feeds the dollar surplus back into the international money market. Those dollars are purchased with foreign currencies, enabling the continuing cash flight to purchase the high-interest-bearing U.S. debt in transactions that swell the dollar reserves in the American banking system. Its policy threatened by the increase in cash reserves, the Federal Reserve Board floats more bonds to get the cash out of the system, keeping interest rates high. The cycle repeats, on and on.

The speculative flights of cash balances, so detrimental in their entry into the American economy, have a devastating effect at their point of exit as well, destabilizing security markets in the country of their origin, and forcing or threatening a collapse of asset values there. To constrain that outflow, countries were obliged to follow the United States in reducing the money supply in their banking systems, tightening credit, and forcing up their rates of interest, thereby closing down opportunities for real domestic investment. Europe, dragged by the flight on international cash balances, followed America down into the deepest and most sustained recession since the Great Depression of the thirties. Thus, the international flight of cash balances subverts the capacity of every nation to control effectively the conditions of the domestic economy. And the concentration of internationally mobile balances in any national financial system renders the economic policy of that nation vulnerable to the constraint and threat of massive cash outflows.

Can the international flight of cash balances, unrelated to real investment or trade in goods and services, be brought under control?

The Selective Control
of International Cash Transactions

A phenomenon so dangerous and destabilizing as the international flight of cash balances is, by the measure of the public interest, without a redeeming grace. I will propose a system of control that I hope will be, not the last, but perhaps the first, word of a discourse.

Building on earlier recommendations, we assume the monetary authority of each country to monopolize all foreign currency transactions in that country.

All domestic cash balances, held by nationals or by others, that derive from cash inflow from abroad or from the sale of imported goods and services would be held apart in regulated accounts separately designated as, say, F-balances. F-balances could be released to be used in domestic transactions under conditions specified by the monetary authority.

Thus, for example, F-balances could be immediately released to purchase goods and services for export or to settle debts on prior exports. They could be used for real investment. They could not be used to purchase government or corporate bonds and securities and other specified assets, except with special dispensation. While control might be subject to evasion, the costs and risks of evasion could effectively deter substantial back-and-forth international movements of cash balances.

PART 5

IS THERE A PREFERRED ALTERNATIVE TO A WORLD SYSTEM OF INTERNATIONAL FREE TRADE?

Memorandum

To: Reader
From: Author
Subject: Is there a preferred alternative to the regime of free trade?

1. Against the benefits of free trade, we balance those of a world system of trade blocs.

2. The trade bloc is modeled after the idea of the European Common Market/European Economic Community; of a free association of states at the same level of development, sharing an outlook and a sense of public purpose, whose economies are merged into an integral market, within which there is complete freedom of trade and mobility of resources, coupled with a system for the formation and implementation of a common economic policy. The market formed through this merger of national economies would be large enough to realize all the economies of large-scale production and specialization, and to enable effective competition between producers at about the same level of technological development. It would be protected against the incursion of foreign imports or investment where such imports or investment is considered destabilizing or in conflict with the common economic policy.

3. A world system of trade blocs would put at risk some, though not all, of the benefits attributed to a regime of free trade. Against that risk, it affords a potential for internal stability and control. A preference for the trade blocs would, in part, depend on the importance attached to a policy for the planned development of the domestic economy.

4. The rational choice of trading systems should take into account a number of issues important for economic development, for example, (a) the scope and character of competition, (b) the flow of investable resources, and (c) the entrapment of a national economy in a lower niche of the ecology of the world industrial system. These issues are discussed and their implications are developed.

15 • Options and Choices

A Shift in Emphasis

Until now, we have raised clear and specific questions concerning our future economic policy, and we have offered concrete, suggestive answers to these. Now, in the consideration and comparison of trade alternatives, the discourse takes a more speculative turn, venturing not to propose and argue for a policy, but rather to clarify the inferences and consequences implicit in choice.

There are no perfect solutions. Whatever solutions there are can be only imperfectly achieved. Every path into the future will have its traps and pitfalls; nevertheless, we can choose between better and worse from among that which is open to us. Here, we invoke the long view to ask whether our goal should be free trade between sovereign nations or some alternative—but what alternative?

The European Common Market/European Economic Community Idea

World War II left as its aftermath one lasting institutional achievement: the European Common Market (ECM) linked with the European Economic Community (EEC). Behind their creation was a magnificent idea, born and nurtured in France. The Common Market would bring together a set of nations, ancient antagonists who nevertheless shared a long history and a basic outlook, and who stood at approximately the same level of technological development. All barriers to trade and investment, competition, labor mobility, and professional intercourse would be removed, creating a market of sufficient size to permit the economies of specialization, mechanization, and large-scale production protected against imports and investments from the outside damaging to the dynamics of its internal development, or that otherwise countervail against the social goals of the community.

The formation and implementation of a coherent policy of social and economic development requires economic governance. For that purpose, the European Economic Community was established to formulate and implement a policy for the planned development and governance of the European Common Market. The ECM/EEC is a community of convenience, a voluntary association whose unity does not depend on any nationalist mystic, but on the general realization of the benefits it offers. It can and has expanded its membership. Quite probably, when its powers of governance are more strongly asserted, there will be member countries who will leave its fold.

Seen from the perspective of things as they were before World War II, the actual achievement of the ECM/EEC has been stupendous. Seen from the perspective of the formative idea, the promise is yet to be fulfilled, especially with regard to the formation of a system of governance able to formulate and implement a coherent and encompassing economic policy for the whole community. Regardless of its current level of achievement, or the mistakes that it has made and its deviations from the path of the founders, the idea of ECM/EEC shines as a beacon on a form of association that might enable a substantial realization of the benefits attributable to a regime of free and balanced trade, without submitting its destiny to the uncertainties and instabilities of international exchange.

Some characteristics of that form of association follow.

1. A set of economies possessed of commensurate infrastructures, factor costs, technologies, and labor standards, as a stable basis for trade and competition, and as a basis for political consensus, would merge into an integral economic entity, that is, a trade bloc.

2. Within the trade bloc, producers would have access to markets of sufficient size to permit all economies of specialization, mechanization, and large-scale production.

3. Within that trade bloc, all barriers to trade and investment, to competition, to labor mobility, and to professional intercourse would be removed.

4. The establishment of the trade bloc would be coupled with the establishment of a system for its economic governance, with powers of

control sufficient to enable the formation and implementation of a coherent policy of economic development.

5. Each trade bloc would operate to promote self-sufficiency, protecting itself from the instabilities and uncertainties of external exchange.

6. Mergers between quite diverse economies whose technologies are not commensurate, but are complementary, would be in order. The essential characteristic of a viable trade bloc is not technological and cultural homogeneity, but a shared policy of economic development.

Thus, as an alternative to the long-range goal of universal freedom of trade and investment, we might conceive a universe of trade blocs, each of a size sufficient to enable all the advantages of specialization, mechanization, and large-scale production. Trade between blocs and coalitions of blocs for their planned, parallel development would be in order.

The Uncertainties of Comparison

We will compare the benefits and detriments of these alternatives: a regime of free international trade versus regulated or negotiated trade between blocs, where each is organized to provide a high degree of self-sufficiency.

We have seen that the benefits of free trade presuppose real exchange, good for good, value for value. The record of actual performance has been, instead, a continuum of imbalance and uncertainty. That, alone, would justify abandoning the aspiration to free trade in favor of the potential for stability and rational control. However, in the contrast and comparison of alternatives in this and the next two chapters, we will assume that the reforms we earlier proposed have been installed in the system of free trade, so that trade is balanced, and the flight of speculative cash balances is effectively controlled. An actual choice, of course, could make no such assumption. Rationally, the choice would rest on a judgment of whether and when the observed detriments of the free trading system might be rectified, and whether and when the envisioned system of trade blocs could be achieved. Such uncertainties would plague any choice between alternative paths to distant goals.

16 • Comparison and Contrast

Two Systems

In this chapter we will compare and contrast the pros and cons of two models or goals for policy. One is a world system of free trade and investment, with no governmental constraint on the movement and exchange of goods, services, and finance; a goal long implicit in the neoclassical economics of ideological liberalism, and pursued with considerable success by the American State Department during the decades after World War II. The other is in the formation of a trade bloc bringing together and merging economies at the same general level of technological development and with comparable factor costs, to operate under common rules and development goals with a shared system of economic governance. Eventually in a world system, each trade bloc would offer an internal market sufficiently large to enable producers to realize the full potentialities of specialization and scale and a broad range of investment opportunities. Each would possess self-sufficiency and autonomy commensurate with balanced economic growth and other development goals.

The one model takes unconstrained entrepreneurial and corporate choice and the mobility of financial resources in international exchange as its value imperative. The other seeks a system of control that would enable a coherent and effective development policy not held hostage by the flux of external choice and event.

The Benefits of International Trade

We return to the old and well-worn questions: Why trade? Why trade between nations? What can be gained from such trade in particular, and from the freedom to trade in general? The uninitiated might think of country A as being more efficient in the production of X, and country B as being more efficient in the production of Y; therefore, they trade X for Y. But gains do not arise simply from the fact that there are differences in the productivities of possible trading partners. If country A is five times more productive in all possibly tradable items than is country B, then there can be no gain from trade between them. Gain from trade requires relative differences in the range of productive capabilities of the parties to the exchange (for example, for B, the production of 2X is equivalent to the production of 1Y, while for A, the production of 2X is equivalent to the production of 1.01Y). The gains from trade will be important only if and inasmuch as there are important differences in their ratios of productivity, item for item.

Hence, the question: Why should there be significant differences between intra-country ratios of productivity?

1. Possibly, because countries are differently endowed by nature.

2. Possibly, because of the advantages of specialization. It is supposed that if country A specializes in the production of X, while country B specializes in the production of Y, this shifts the productivity ratio sharply in favor of X in country A, and of Y in country B. Country A will have realized the economies of specialization in X. Country B will have realized the economies of specialization in Y. Hence, a larger, aggregated XY product can, through trade, be shared between them. But, note: The key assumption here (an assumption implicit in Adam Smith's argument for freedom of trade) is that only through international trade can A or B have access to a market sufficiently large to enable the economies of specialization via large-scale production.

3. Possibly, because of idiosyncratic variations in productive capabilities, and because of a lag in or barriers to the dissemination of knowledge and skills.

These, then, are the three possible reasons for intra-economy differences in productivity ratios as the basis for gains through trade: (1) variation in the bounties and burdens of nature, (2) the economies of specialization, and (3) idiosyncratic variation in the acquisition and lag in the dissemination of knowledge and skill. The question is whether, or to what degree, these sources of variance and the benefits of trade to be derived from them would be put at risk through the transformation of a system of free trade to one of trade blocs.

The emphasis of economics in explaining the benefits to be gained through international trade is on the advantages that accrue through country-by-country specialization. The benefits are functions not of international trade but of large-scale production. In a trade bloc where the domestic market is of sufficient size to enable all the gains of specialization, mechanization, and large-scale production, there cannot be, on that account, any gains from international trade.

The benefits of trade derive also from variations in natural advantage, which are of greater or lesser importance depending on the intrinsic necessity, replaceability, or substitutability of the items traded. It will be less to the extent that the economies of the trade blocs encompass a range of climatic variations and resource availabilities, and as science develops synthetic substitutes.

A system of separate trade blocs where each seeks the autonomy required for its development goals does not rule out trade. Trade would certainly enable the importation of goods and resources from regions in possession of a natural advantage. It is rather trade based on idiosyncratic advantages that would be at least partially excluded as a matter of political choice when judged to be in conflict with goals of internal economic stability and development. Hence it is the risks to the benefits of trade based on idiosyncratic advantage that a rational preference for a system of free trade rather than of trade blocs must rely. Trade in goods and services reflecting idiosyncratic advantages would not be precluded in a system of trade blocs, though it well might, as a matter of political choice, be excluded where it conflicted with the goals of stability and economic autonomy. The book of economics is silent concerning idiosyncratic variations as a basis for trade, perhaps because neither the benefits nor their source can be quantified or generalized. They are important nevertheless and might indeed be difficult to accommodate in regulated trade between blocs. What should be clearly understood is that since they are based on a knowledge that can be learned and a practice that can be acquired, idiosyncratic advantages should be and are essentially transitory. They should be and are more or less continuously wiped out and reacquired through the dissemination of technology on the one side and through the creative advance and development of new technologies on the other: twin processes that adapt to either trading system. The free trade benefits at risk must be balanced against the advantages offered by the trade bloc in enabling the control of variables critical in the formation and implementation of a policy for internal economic development including the elimination of the instabilities and uncertainties that free trade introduces into the domestic economies of the trading nations and that cannot be removed by any reform of the mechanics of the system. For example, when bad policies produce a depression in country A, to the degree that A is a market for the goods produced by countries B, C, and D, those countries will have the problem of production instability and unemployment thrust upon them as the consequence of policies other than their own. Other values of economic autonomy will be discussed in chapter 17.

17 • Policy Implications

This chapter focuses on some problems and considerations important in a choice between trading systems.

The Scope of Competition

It can be argued that a regime of free trade and investment, by broadening the effective market, provides a check on monopoly; and, in widening the scope of competition, stimulates efficiency and innovation.

Victory in such a competition however, may be the consequence not of comparative productivities, but of transitory variation in exchange rates, or of differences in the power of capital to force down labor's share of the national product. A potential virtue of the trade bloc is in enabling competition between (and in confining competition to) entities with the same labor standards, factor costs, infrastructure, and level of technology in order to secure a stable and balanced path of development. The trade bloc does not exclude competition by international corporations establishing subsidiaries or organizing operations in trade blocs other than their own.

The Disposition of Investable Resources

It can be argued that free trade and investment would spontaneously allocate resources to those industries and those regions of the world where the highest risk-discounted yield on investment is available; hence, optimizing the net contribution of new investment to the general increase in world GNP.

Suppose that, indeed, under a regime of free international trade and investment, investment was allocated to obtain the highest possible risk-discounted yield; the highest yield on investment is not to be equated with the optimal contribution to production and productivity. Such investment may have as its objective not to increase production, nor to raise productivity, nor to improve the quality of production, nor to produce a different product. It may, for example, be undertaken to relocate operations from where labor is organized and high wages are paid to where labor is unorganized and is more exploitable. Profits are made, not by producing better, but by reducing labor's share.

In the United States, a substantial part of American industrial investment has been, and currently is, devoted to shifting the locus of production for the American market from the unionized, high-wage shops and factories in the North to the more vulnerable labor in the South and Southwest; from there to Mexico, Honduras, Haiti, Korea, and Taiwan. For each shift there are heavy social costs and painful dislocations. Each is a movement from greater to lesser efficiency and from higher to lower productivity. The result is waste, instability, lower productivity, and a widening of the income gap between wage earners and profit takers.

Such investment is subversive of any income policy, especially when what is sought is an economy that generates high and rising wages and a labor force protected by independent trade unions. It could hardly be checked or controlled under a regime of free international trade and investment.

To Whom Does the Investable Surplus Belong?

An economy produces a surplus available for investment. The disposition of that surplus is of critical importance for technological advance and industrial development. It may convey benefits far beyond, and of greater significance than, those that are reaped by the profit takers, who, in a free market economy, normally exercise the investment choice. These "external economies," over and above the gains reaped by the profit takers, will accrue to the economy in which the surplus is invested, for example, in the benefits of an upgraded infrastructure attracting other industrial investment and accelerating development throughout; in higher wages, new employment, and career opportunities for labor; in sales and production opportunities for a network of suppliers, contractors, subcontractors, builders, transporters, and so forth; in a rise in tax revenues and, hence, the greater availability of public service. What if the profit takers should decide under a regime of free international trade and investment to invest the surplus, not in the economy where it was produced, but in some other?

A society's economy produces a surplus available for investment. The future strength of that society depends on where and how that surplus is invested. To whom belongs the fundamental right to dispose of that surplus? Consider the case of Great Britain in the nineteenth and early twentieth centuries. She was then the great free trader and free investor in the international economy, just as the United States has been during the decades after World War II. Through force of arms and the power of diplomacy, Great Britain supported, and through its tax system subsidized, the investment overseas of the surplus produced by the British economy, just as the United States has done for the surplus produced by the U.S. economy during the decades following World War II. British investment then, as American investment subsequently, moved to the four corners of the world in hot pursuit of the highest possible yields as income for those profit takers who possessed the power to direct the flow of investment. Where weaker people sought to fend off the incursion, gunboats were sent to blast open the way for its sacred flow. So, in its turn, the United States has used its arms and its diplomacy to keep open or to force open foreign doors to the entry of free enterprise and the American dollar.

Who benefited from the massive overseas investment of the surplus produced by the British economy? Not British industry. Its decaying plant and obsolete equipment was soon surpassed by the industry of those nations into which Britain had poured its investment. Not the British economy. Not the British worker. There were, however, beneficiaries: a race of beautiful idlers living in graceful and unparalleled luxury on the untaxed incomes of ancestral investment overseas. It was the societies wherein the investment had been made that reaped the external economies upon which technological and industrial development depends. The critical benefits of British investment in Argentina accrued not to the British, but to the Argentine, economy. The critical benefits of American investment in Germany accrued not to the American, but to the German, economy. When the resources of a nation are preempted for the purpose of investment, who should have first claim to their fruits?

To whom does the investable surplus belong? We know who now controls the investable surplus: corporate elites, bankers, financiers, the very wealthy. But who produced it? Who, in the moral sense, has the right to claim the benefits of its use? That surplus is the joint product of those who labor, manage, educate, govern, and of science and whatever is the source of creative technological change. Perhaps least of all is it the product of those who control its disposition.

If the society as a whole that generated an investable surplus has a prior right to the external benefits of investment made with that surplus, it is denied that right in a regime of free investment. Then the investable resource can be siphoned off to benefit only a small segment of the society to the detriment of the rest. The value of a trade bloc in this regard would be to enable the development of an economy with real investment opportunities of a breadth and diversity sufficient to enable the full and efficient disposition of the investable surplus produced by that economy, and that would, except under special public dispensation and collective rule, confine the disposition of the investable surplus to the economy of the trade bloc that produced it.

The Transfer of Technology

It can also be argued that a regime of free international trade and free international investment, coupled with the operation of the international corporation, provides a powerful instrument for the dissemination and transfer of technology. This has been demonstrated by the amazing rapidity with which whole new industries, traditionally generations in the making, in steel, machine tools, shipbuilding, and petrochemicals, have been established anew and in full modernity in third world countries.

No doubt the transfer of technology has been served through exports embodying new technology, and by the wholesale transfer of advanced industrial operations through international investment and the export of services. Nothing in a system of trade blocs precludes such transfers. Such transfers rather would support the goals of the trade bloc which would benefit from importing new technology and whose domestic economy would not be threatened by the export of technologies of its own. The motivation for the direct and complete transfer of technology should be stronger in a world system of trade blocs than under a regime of free trade. Those of a trade bloc who seek to capitalize on a new technology in their possession and who are denied the opportunity to export the product of that technology, would have no option but to choose a more potent means of transfer by offering to sell or lease the information to other trade blocs, or to establish its operation there themselves. Inasmuch as the economies of the trade blocs are autonomous and do not depend on or interact with each other, the transfer of technological information will be less constrained than under a regime of free trade and investment; since, to that degree, the technology could be transferred or its operation could be established elsewhere without the fear that its product would return as a competitive import. Research centers and the corporate research and development operations set apart in different trade blocs could cooperate in research and share its fruits without the fear that in so doing they might lose competitive advantage.

Fixed into the Niches
of the International Trading System

Suppose that in a world of free international trade the trading nations concentrate their production in areas where they possess comparative advantage, and that such comparative advantage is based upon idiosyncratic variations in technological mastery acquired as a matter of historical happenstance. Suppose that therefore aggregated production costs are less and world prices are lower than they otherwise would have been. Now suppose the world economy consists of countries A, B, and C. Country A having a historical advantage in science and engineering produces all of whatever requires a science-based technology. Country B through the particularities of its cultural development has acquired greater skills in organization and finance and hence produces all that requires complex organizational and financial skills. Country C is left with the residual. It does what requires stoop labor in the fields, toil with the needle and the sewing machine in the cottages, pick and shovel work in the mines. Even though this arrangement on the whole produces more at a lower cost so that "the consumer" is better off, can it really be supposed, no matter whether the consumer buys for less, that there is no better alternative for the people of country C? Alas, under a regime of free trade, the people of C would have no other choice. This is the niche into which they have been forced, into which they are fixed, and where they must remain.

Who, then, is the consumer "made better off"? For there are consumers and consumers, would-be consumers and once-were consumers and never-became consumers, here or there, down below or high above. Nor are we simply consumers, or even primarily consumers. The work we do, or that we are cut off from doing, matters. We have, or we might have had, hopes and aspirations, depending on where our economy is going, what it is becoming, and hence, on the opportunities it provides or that it cannot provide. That matters. It matters whether we, concerned for one another, can take a hand in determining what our economy becomes, on what will be the balance and range of opportunities it offers to our people and the avenues it opens to choice and to change. When the economy is forced and fixed into a niche under a regime of free international trade and investment, these are matters significantly excluded from the realm of social choice.

The corporation is a system. The economy is a system. In these systems there are niches. As classes, as operations, as individuals, we occupy those niches, and those niches define and determine our prerogatives, our powers, our independence, our breadth of expression, our opportunity to communicate, to relate to others, to learn. There are dead-end niches, and others where the avenues of advance are wide and open. There are niches to be preferred, sought for, fought for. There are others to be shunned and avoided; once fixed in those caverns of despair, it may be difficult, even impossible, to escape from them.

The economy of international trade is also a system with niches for whole nations or regions, niches to be preferred, niches to be dreaded; niches into which the national economy, once fixed, perhaps cannot ever escape. Free trade absorbs the economies of the nations into its entrails, and assigns them to niches of specialization; niches that define and determine their prerogatives, their power, their share of the common output, their independence, their dominion over or their subordination to others, their opportunities to become, to develop, to advance. Free trade and investment, in fixing nations into the niches of a system, constrain the right and power of a society to explore, to develop, and to possess a preferred range of variations, a preferred balance of specializations.

The economy ought to be, and should be, designed as an engine for change and development. A shift of energies into, and a building upon the variations within its domain, is the principle of social mutation.

The capacity of a society to become, to adapt, to evolve, to transcend itself, depends on the nuclei of variations that it possesses. Variations and the capacity for mutation they convey are wiped out through the concentrations enforced under a regime of free trade and investment.

For more than two centuries, international trade has relegated the peoples of the third world into niches deprived of the dynamic that elsewhere was the source of revolutionary change and development. They were fixed into the niche of stagnation and deprivation by the export drive of those others who possessed a superior technology and organization. Inferiority of technology and organization is not indigenous to any economy or society. Relative technological superiority or inferiority is not a stable basis for mutual gain through exchange. It is, and should be, a transitory state, a stage in the process wherein the superior technology is learned, acquired, assimilated, and transcended. The onslaught of foreign competition based on the advantages of a superior technology and a greater skill in organization may be a spur to learning, to the advance of technology, to the improvement of organization. It can also destroy the industrial base, wipe out established layers of skills, eliminate the nuclei of variation that constitute the capacity for learning and development, abort all possibility of pursuing an avenue of technological advance, and retrogress the economy to an inferior niche in the ecological system of world industry. India is a case in point.

In the nineteenth century, India was opened to the regime of free trade and investment. Imports from Western Europe, the United States, and Japan flooded its markets. Foreign investors and exporters benefited. Some consumers in India benefited. An ancient and highly evolved artisan base that could have been the nucleus and vehicle for learning and technological advance was wiped out. The village economy was destroyed. A relatively affluent and productive people was transformed into an economy of coolie labor at the lowest and most impoverished rung of the world's trading system.

The United States has already experienced a devastating industrial decline. There has been a closing of the doors of opportunity and of learning, a shutting off of avenues of development. Under a true regime of free trade, the great bastions of our industrial prowess would by now have collapsed. The work force drifts downward into the waste and idleness of an underclass, or to become garage attendants, dishwashers, male nurses, and busboys in the service industries. These are matters that transcend the interests of the consumer as measured by the prices paid for imported products. It is time to pause and consider the kind of society and economy we shall become.

The Underdeveloped Countries of the World

What impact would a general reorientation of policy toward the formation of autonomous trade blocs, each seeking a degree of autarky, have on the underdeveloped countries of the world? The technically advanced could, just as now, give the third world a helping hand. Indeed, technical assistance would be less constrained than it would under a regime of free trade, for it could be offered without the fear of nurturing a competition damaging to the home industry.

The underdeveloped countries would be deprived, it is true, of random incursions of investment by firms from advanced industrial societies seeking to produce low-cost exports for shipment back to their own home markets by exploiting an unorganized and vulnerable labor force. But the currents of world trade would no longer dictate for those countries an inferior niche in an ecological system of world industry. They would be left to go it alone, form their own trade bloc or not, succeed or fail—on their own.

A very insightful young person wrote to me:

> My thesis . . . comes out of a review of the different theories of development; the infallible recipes for takeoff etc., which hail from the North, and the endless whines of protest, explaining why development is morally and economically impossible, which come from the South. There are two different outlooks on development; from the North underdevelopment is seen as a marvelous opportunity; a flower about to burst into bloom, and from the South it is viewed as the eternal victim of somebody else's over watering or under-fertilizing. I think the optimism/pessimism difference is the key. The fact that the Third World sees itself as a martyr rather than as a new frontier says it all.

I believe what she says is true: an outlook, a point of view is at the heart of the problem, but it is an outlook formed by the niche these societies have for centuries occupied in the international trading system; one of dependence, subordination, and inferiority. In a world of autonomous trading blocs, countries of the third world would be for the first time on their own; responsible for themselves. They would be faced with the enormous problem of finding an inner coherence, of raising their domestic markets to a mass propensity to consume commensurate with their latent power to produce; an overwhelming problem, but one whose solution would lift them at last from the cycle of underdevelopment.

Japan and Us

Perhaps the issue can be brought home with the following example. It would seem the Japanese are now better than we are in every industrial technology oriented to the satisfaction of civilian wants and needs. Not that much better; we can produce good automobiles, steel, machine tools, ships, cameras, radios, television sets, computers, on and on. Their superiority is not set in stone, any more than ours was in the recent past. We can, we are, learning from them as earlier they learned from us. Nevertheless it can be reasonably hypothesized that in the present context, theirs is sufficiently superior that if trade were truly and fully free, the products of Japanese technology would wipe out and replace ours, not only in international, but also in our own domestic market. In a balanced, hence sustainable trade relationship, they would sell us the products of advanced technology. We would send them what could be taken from our soil, our mines, and our forest.

Proud America would have slipped into the third world niche of the international trading system. Cumulatively, the Japanese would become more firmly entrenched in their niche, where high tech breeds its own succession. We would become more deeply buried and lost in ours.

Is this a scenario that we or any other nation should freely choose? Or would we prefer to keep our options open, to preserve the spread of individual opportunity and sustain the possibility of industrial regeneration in the autonomy of a trade bloc?

PART 6

WHAT POLICY CAN CONFRONT THE DEPLETION AND ULTIMATE EXHAUSTION OF A CRITICAL NATURAL RESOURCE?

Memorandum

To: Reader
From: Author
Subject: What policy is there for the depletion of a resource?

1. At the root of our environmental problems are ingrained but false perceptions of reality: of the earth as a bottomless well from which the benefits of nature can be endlessly pumped, and of the air and oceans as a depthless sewer into which the wastes and poisons of industry can be endlessly dumped. Alas, the sewer is backing up, the well is running dry.

2. Hotteling's neoclassical analysis demonstrates that under conditions of pure and perfect competition, an exhaustible resource would be doled out over time in a manner that maximized the realized value of the asset to ownership and of the utility to be derived from the use of the resource by consumers, until the disaster of total exhaustion. The historical movements of price and rates of depletion have no discernible relation to this theory. Leaving resource depletion to the market is to leave it to chance and happenstance.

3. For more than a century, the United States was the major source and supplier of cheap crude oil to the world, until 1973–74, when output leveled off, and thereafter (in the territory of the original forty-eight states) steadily declined. This event spurred a twin realization: (1) The well was not bottomless. What happened in the United States must, given the magnitude of oil consumption in an industrializing world, happen elsewhere, eventually everywhere, hence, oil reserves should be husbanded. This realization led, to the formation of OPEC and the shattering rise in the price of oil. (2) The United States, now the world's major importer of oil, was vulnerable in the politics of petroleum. This realization led to the Arab oil embargo.

4. Because we failed to understand that nothing can increase the production of what nature produced eons ago, our political response to America's vulnerability was an effort to increase the domestic *production* of petroleum by (1) imposing quotas on the import of oil from Arabia and other distant lands, and (2) offering for lease or sale at bargain basement prices drilling rights on our national land reserves. In the name of national security, we accelerated the depletion of safe, American reserves, thereby increasing American vulnerability to a cutoff of imports.

5. The end of the road, where it will require more energy to obtain a barrel of oil than is to be obtained from that barrel of oil, is in sight. There is no rational answer to the question of how fast to deplete, for that is to ask whether it is better to die after a slow decline into deep poverty, or to live it up big and die quick with a bang. What needs to be asked is not how soon to die, but how to survive. Survival requires the development of a beneficent energy alternative to fossil fuels.

That is a critical task for the modern state, indeed for the consortium of states, since the same problem is shared by all, and the same solution would save them all.

6. American experience in this regard is a case study of the frustration and failure of a weak and timid political system, dominated by borrowed businessmen, infected with fear of creeping socialism, kowtowing to the fancied omni-competence of the market.

18 • Perceptions

History can be understood as a tale of perceptions formed and failed. A people comes to understand its social world in a way that is rooted in experience and is in accord with experience. This way of understanding its world is elaborated by its intellectuals, who iron out its contradictions and formulate its rationale. Inculcated in the home and in the school and on the street, into the mode of thinking of successive generations, it is incorporated into the culture, into the law, and into policy. It is accepted as truth. And for a time and a place, it may be close to the truth. But what is true today will be less true tomorrow. For our world is changing. As it changes, the truth of established belief diminishes. Between the perceived and the actual, the gap widens. The accepted, inculcated social hypothesis fails. Problems can no longer be resolved within its frame. It itself becomes the problem. The commitment to its truth becomes a commitment to falsehood. The grooves of established thought become a pit. An escape from the pit may be required for survival.

Then the agenda for survival needs more than the analysis of policy problems and proposals for their solution. Behind those problems, and at their causal roots, are modes of thinking that distort the real, and stand foursquare as the barriers to every rational solution. It is the false imageries, the obsolete ideologies, the inculcated prisms of perception, that blinker vision and distort rather than reveal, that must be uprooted. That surely has been a lesson of this book in its survey of these critical policy problems: depression, inflation, stagflation, technological decline, lagging productivity, failing competitiveness, and instability, imbalance, and policy impotence in international trade. At the roots of each of these is a mode of thinking that must be overcome to reach the field of rational choice.

Consider some of the common fallacies that stand as barriers to rational choice.

The Fallacy of Sovereign Individualism

Sovereign individualism is a noble idea, formulated centuries ago, expressed in the *Rights of Man*, in the United States Constitution, in the *Wealth of Nations*. It envisages society as a universe of autonomous individuals, self-responsible, self-sufficient, self-seeking, self-deciding; and the economy as an endless grid. Every individual or business firm (with the firm always understood as the instrument of the entrepreneurial individual) occupies a space of freedom, of autonomy, on the grid; a space marked out by the prerogatives of property and the rights of man. There, in the search for self-betterment, each person or business firm is, by its own volition, for its own purposes, engaged in a competitive interaction as a buyer-seller, consumer-producer, employer-employee.

It is not my intention to deny the value of the individual, or to suppose that this idea does not correspond with some aspects of our experience. But armed only with this perception, we cannot begin to comprehend or deal with critical phenomena in a society where the key decision-taking entities are not individuals but organizations. We cannot begin to understand the place and character of autonomous organization in the formation of economic policy with regard, for example, to the phenomenon of stagflation, nor how in its permutations, the lengthening organizational distance between the locus of control and that of operation, and the phenomenon of conglomeration, throws the balance of power into the hands of asset manipulators and helps explain the extraordinary decline of American industry.

The Omni-Competent Market
and the Omni-Competent State

Coupled with the fallacy of sovereign individualism, indeed following from it, is the fallacy of the omni-competent market, and conversely, the blind bias against the state, against collective in contrast to individual choice that can be called the fallacy of creeping socialism. Such certainly is now the prevailing mode of thought in the United States and Great Britain. But as one moves East and back but a few decades in time, that perception shaded into and finally became its polar opposite in the Soviet Union and China: the fallacy of the omni-competent state, coupled with a blind bias against individualized endeavor. In the 1980s, the nations of the East have been struggling to escape the omni-competent state, while in the West, the omni-competence of the market has been proclaimed with fanatic zeal. Both are fallacious. But we speak now of the West, and it is therefore with the fallacies of market omni-competence and of creeping socialism that we must deal.

In the vision projected of an omni-competent market, the free and autonomous movement of price controls the behavior of every individual and business firm, and guides resources surely and swiftly into their most productive use; a far cry from market realities. Armed only with this idea, it is impossible to comprehend the phenomena of depression, mass unemployment, stagflation, the decline of the American system, the continuum of imbalance in international trade, the roots of underdevelopment, or the systemic character of an international trade that captures and holds some national economies fixed into niches of despair. A blind bias against the state stands in the way of understanding collective choice and its instruments as neither sacred nor diabolic, but as the only possible agency for dealing with critical problems of the whole.

Our focus in this chapter is on natural resources, and more specifically on energy. In a review of energy policy, we will again encounter the fallacies of sovereign individualism, of market omni-competence and creeping socialism as barriers to the field of rational choice, and of other failures of perception as well; particularly, what we will call the fallacy of the bottomless well.

The Bottomless Well and the Depthless Sewer

The false perception is that the resources of the earth can be dredged up as from a bottomless well, and that the air and the oceans are as a depthless sewer into which all wastes and residues can mindlessly be dumped; that nature will rearrange what modern technology ceaselessly and ever more powerfully disarranges.

In Kenneth Boulding's words:

> Earth has become a "spaceship" and a very small, crowded spaceship at that, destination unknown. Up to now the human race has behaved and acted as if it lived on an illimitable plain. Now the earth has be-

come a sphere, and we have to think of society as a sociosphere; that is, a sphere of all human interaction; and in this respect a sphere is very different from a plain. The great plains are gone for good: that was an episode and a very brief episode in human history, and we will probably never be able to go through it again.

In the spaceship there are no mines, no ores, no fossil fuels, no pollutable reservoirs, and no sewers. Everything has to be recycled, the water to go through the kidneys and algae to the kidneys and algae, and so on indefinitely. Everything has to go from man to his environment, from the environment back to man . . . from now on the spaceship is beginning to close in on us. From the point of view of pollution, this may be much closer than we think.[1]

The bottomless well is running dry. The depthless sewer is backing up. The very biosystem that rearranges what we ceaselessly disarrange is endangered.

Note

1. Boulding, Kenneth E. "The Prospect of Economic Abundance." *The Control of the Environment.* Nobel Conference. (Amsterdam: North Holland Press), 1966.

19 • Problems and Policies

The Depletion of a Resource

Unlike the problems of policy dealt with earlier, the problems of energy do not entirely derive from failures of perception. They are also rooted in two simple physical facts: depletion and pollution. Our emphasis here will be on depletion.

We drive our cars, we heat our homes, we light our cities, we fuel our aircraft and the machines in our factories; we have based our industry, indeed our lives, on the use of certain natural resources: coal, natural gas, and especially petroleum. Modern industry and the modern economy consume the limited stocks of these resources, devouring them with enormous rapidity. As the stock is depleted, what remains buried somewhere in the bowels of the earth becomes more difficult to find, more costly to recover, until at last it is gone as a viable source of energy.

We will explain and critique the policy responses to the brute fact of depletion. If ultimately we fail to spell out what specifically should be done, we have answers enough to the question: What ought to be avoided? While the American experience will be our case in point, to a remarkable degree the rest of the world has followed the same policy path and demonstrated the same misconceptions. Our review of this experience will demonstrate the pernicious effects upon policy of those fallacies of perception: market omni-competence, creeping socialism, and the bottomless well.

Depletion and the Market

To many of the faithful, the omni-competence of the market is not subject to challenge, nor to question. We can ask them how the market would deal with resource depletion.

Decades ago, in his "Economics of Exhaustible Resources," Harold Hotelling published the definitive neoclassical market analysis of resource depletion.[1] Hotelling's model assumes pure and perfect competition, that is, an unbounded number of buyers and sellers, where each competitor is fully informed concerning the parameters of choice, where each seller acts to maximize the net value of his assets through decisions to sell or withhold from sale not only his stocks of the exhaustible resource (petroleum), but also the drilling rights, the proven reserves, and the active wells in his possession. The owner must make this key decision: whether to sell off his stock at current prices, or to retain his stock in anticipation of higher prices later. That choice determines the rate of depletion. In this decision, three variables are brought into play: the current price of petroleum, its anticipated future price, and the rate of interest. The rate of interest indicates the opportunity cost of holding back on the sale and depletion of existing stocks, for it is a measure of what could have been earned by reinvesting the income received from their depletion and sale. When the rate of interest goes up, rapid depletion becomes more profitable. Conversely, when there is a rise in the anticipated future price of petroleum, it becomes more attractive to reduce current depletion in order to hold reserves for future sale at higher prices.

There can be no constant equilibrium price or rate of depletion, since all ongoing depletion must change the prospect of future scarcity. When a rise in interest rates induces more rapid depletion, the accelerated exhaustion of stocks leads to the rational expectation of greater future scarcity, hence the anticipation of higher future prices. These counterbalanced forces determine the actual rate of depletion, always at the point where ownership maximizes the discounted income to be gained from either depleting or reserving the stocks in their possession. Thus, according to Hotelling, the limited stock of the available resource would be doled out over time so as to maximize both the realized value of the assets of those in possession, and of the utility attributable to the use of the resource.

From Hotelling, one can deduce a number of interesting points:

1. For an exhaustible resource, in this instance crude oil, the question is not, How much shall we produce? All that can be produced has already been produced. The question is only, How rapidly shall we exhaust, use up, deplete, what nature produced eons ago? The decision can serve only to increase or decrease the rate of

depletion. It is a matter of timing. Should the resource be used up today or reserved for tomorrow? More now and less later? Less now and more later?

2. The logic of market choice would be the same, and the price of oil and the rate of depletion would be quite the same, with an infinite number of competitors under conditions of pure and perfect competition, as when all petroleum was controlled by a single rational and informed monopolist. It would appear that under the aegis of corporate oligopoly, the pre-OPEC pricing of oil ran counter to the neoclassical welfare criterion, in being too low and in depleting an exhaustible resource too rapidly.

3. Hotelling's market of informed and rational choice, were it obtainable, might afford a more ordered, even a preferable, path to a point of social disaster. The theory says nothing about surviving the disaster of resource exhaustion.

4. To leave the depletion choice to the actual market is, in fact, to leave it to drift and happenstance. Actual, observed behavior in the oil markets of the world has in no way approximated the logic of Hotelling's model of informed and rational choice. Thus, for example, when the real rate of interest (the nominal rate outpaced by inflation) fell to zero in the 1970s, while the prospect of future scarcity increased with every passing day, instead of a virtual cessation of the pumping of oil from the earth, as the "logic" of the market would dictate, the rise in oil consumption and the worldwide depletion of crude oil reserves continued unabated.

The actual movements of oil prices, radically erratic, discontinuous, and unrelated to the changes in the real rate of interest, cannot be explained by neoclassical theory. There are good reasons why crude oil pricing and depletion rates do not follow this market logic or, perhaps, any other discernible rationale. Each enterprise operates in a frame of ineradicable uncertainty and pervasive ignorance of the critical parameters of the depletion choice. Indeed, given the dispersed ownership of that global resource, it is never possible for the individual enterprise to know, or reasonably to assess the actual availability of ultimately extractable reserves, let alone to foresee future demand.

There were circumstances, moreover, that biased choice in favor of rapid depletion. Large integrated companies with drilling rights, or possessing proven reserves, in poor, newly independent countries of the third world were constantly pressed to surrender a larger proportion of their oil revenues to the host government and/or were threatened with nationalization. Presumably, they were impelled to make the best of their situations by getting the oil out as rapidly as possible before the terms of the contracts with their host countries worsened, or before they lost possession entirely. Even where they were secure in their ownership of the resource, their interest was not only in maximizing its value as an asset over the period of its depletion. They also had a counterbalancing interest in the profits earned in maintaining a high-volume throughput of the oil via their refining and distribution networks.

The Depletion of American Petroleum Reserves

Consider the American experience. For a century in the territory of the original forty-eight states, America was the world's major source, producer, consumer, exporter, of petroleum. It supplied the world with cheap crude oil. Each year, year after year, more oil was "discovered," more was "produced," more was exported. Then, in 1973–74, output leveled off. As was inevitable from the beginning, the volume of production began to decline. In spite of an unprecedented rise in the price of oil, in spite of a quantum increase in the oil wells drilled and in spending on oil exploration, drilling, and recovery, that decline continues. From its original role of the great exporter, the United States has become the major importer of crude oil.

The great exporter had become the great importer of crude oil. The United States was dependent, and each year was growing more dependent, on imports of oil from abroad. The sea lanes were vulnerable. The lands whence the oil was imported were distant, vulnerable, and not very friendly. How should we respond to the fact of dependence?

The first response, under President Eisenhower, was to impose import quotas that sharply reduced oil imports. Import quotas remained in force from the turn of the 1950s until the 1970s. It was supposed that by reducing imports of the low-priced crude oil from Arabia and other distant lands, the domestic price of oil in the United States would rise, and that would stimulate and increase the *production* of petroleum in the United States. This rise in domestic production would protect the United States against any cutoff of oil imports, and preserve American autonomy from externally imposed constraints.

How strangely perverse was this policy. It thought only of production. It forgot the brute fact of depletion. The United States "protected" itself by accelerating the depletion of its safe, domestic oil reserves, of the reserves that would be available in time of crisis; correspondingly slowing down the depletion of distant reserves in unfriendly hands. Its effect, in accelerating the depletion of domestic reserves, was cumulatively to increase American dependence on imports, and consequently, its industrial and military vulnerability.

In all the decades from the administration of President Eisenhower to that of President Nixon, not a voice was raised in Congress or the Senate, or by any public official, president, or member of his staff, or by any economist or any other academic, to protest a system of quotas that in the name of national security accelerated the depletion of safe reserves, leaving the United States and its allies high and dry in the face of the Arab oil embargo.[2] Could there be a clearer demonstration of the fallacy of the bottomless well, abetted by that of an omnicompetent market? The formation of American energy policy never ceased to be filtered through those twin fallacies.

In 1982 James Watt (and later his successors), as secretary of the interior, expressing the policy of President Reagan, with the concurrence of Congress, promoted the sale at bargain prices of oil drilling rights to the great tracts of national forest and national wilderness, and of oil drilling rights to the whole continental shelf at the edge of the American landmass. Turning over the last of our protected oil reserves to corporate enterprise would, it was argued, induce an increase in the domestic *production* of oil, and thereby render us less dependent on foreign imports. Again, trusting to the omni-competent market and relying on the assumption of a bottomless well, a policy is embraced, justified in the name of national defense to accelerate the depletion of our safe domestic oil reserves, making it absolutely certain that in times of crisis, even less of the resource would be available to satisfy priority needs.

A heralded article by an MIT professor sums up the standard outlook.[3] To forestall creeping socialism, he would forbid any intervention by the state in the operation of the omni-competent market for the purpose of developing alternative energy sources. He would bolster America's capacity to withstand any cutoff of imports from abroad by imposing a tariff on imports of petroleum. Instead of quotas, a tariff; but the logic is exactly the same. A tariff would raise the domestic price of petroleum, hence the profits realized on the sale of oil from American wells. That would induce corporate enterprise to *produce* more oil in the United States, as though oil could be pumped endlessly but more rapidly from a bottomless well.

Given ignorance and uncertainty, and given also that for a while (a very short while in the life of societies) there was a linear increase in the quantities of crude oil being pumped from the earth, the fallacy of the bottomless well prevailed. Policy, blind to the realities of depletion, turned on the costs of production. The continuing decline of oil output in the United States, for long the prime supplier to the world, drove home the twin realizations that (1) depletion was real and had to be taken into account, and (2) the United States, now dependent on imports and no longer able to supply its allies, was vulnerable in the politics of oil. It was the first realization, plus the knowledge that the United States could no longer dominate oil pricing, that led OPEC, the association of oil producers comprised mostly of third world countries, to plan the constraints on their production and the consequent shattering rise in petroleum prices. The second realization led to the Arab oil embargo.

OPEC Prices and the American Consumer

The slackening and decline in America's output of petroleum, after so many years of continuous increase when the United States had been the great supplier and exporter of cheap crude oil, was a signal to the world that what had happened here would happen there, that depletion was real and inescapable, that the well was not bottomless, that reserves of oil must be husbanded and doled out carefully over time. OPEC responded by slowing down its depletion rates. With less oil forthcoming, the price of imported oil in the United States increased by more than 600 percent. Aside from the price effect, substantially less of the critical and ubiquitous energy resource was available. We were, as a people, poorer than we were before. The question then was how to share the burden of greater poverty.

At that time, oil and natural gas prices in the United States were partially controlled under a long-established species of regulation designed to protect the consumer against the power of natural monopoly. Under the then prevailing rule, the price of oil and natural gas from so-called old wells already in operation was held at a level that covered operating and investment costs plus a fair return on investment. The price of oil from new wells, that is, all oil wells discovered and drilled after a threshold date, was not controlled. Therefore the regulations then in force could not affect incentives to explore for and drill new wells.

Under those circumstances, the oil companies, their earnings from the old wells unabated, and cashing in on the soaring price of the output of new wells, were enormously enriched even under the conditions of general impoverishment. Consumers, obliged to pay those higher prices and make do with less, were worse off than before. However, including the controlled price of domestic crude (from old wells) in the average charged at the gas pump eased the deprivation visited upon consumers.

The response of the American government to this crisis of soaring import prices was to abandon domestic regulation entirely and allow an unbounded upward movement in the price of domestic oil and natural gas. The whole pot was turned over to the oil companies. It was the largest transfer of income from poorer to richer in living memory. Why?

It cannot be explained or justified as an encouragement to the exploration and drilling for new oil and gas, since the price of oil and gas from new wells had not been controlled. Even if the price of oil from both new and old wells had been controlled, exploration and new drilling could have been encouraged without decontrol by subsidizing deep drilling or through a research and development program to develop techniques to reduce the cost of exploration and drilling. Or, if the objective was to equate the domestic and imported price of crude, that could have been done by imposing a tax on the controlled wellhead price of the oil and natural gas produced in the United States. Then, rather than accruing to the oil companies, a part of the great price windfall would have been siphoned off as public revenue, allowing a compensating decrease in other taxes.

Total decontrol can be explained only as a kowtow to the idol of market omni-competence.

The "Stockhole"

The experience of the Arab embargo raised the awareness of a national vulnerability to a sudden cessation of oil imports. I like to think that it was Mr. Schlesinger, President Carter's secretary of energy, who had the inspiration. He puffs at his pipe and ponders the need for some margin of safety that could, in the face of another oil embargo, at least enable a time for adjustment. And the light dawns. Of course! Exhausted oil wells had left great holes in the earth. Let the government buy petroleum from private companies, pump it down those holes, then pump it back out again to meet the needs of the country in times of crisis. Presto, the problem was solved. The country would have its safety ''stockhole.''

That became, and that remains, the policy of the United States: to purchase petroleum pumped out of one hole in the ground, transship it, all at great expense, and pump it back into another hole in the ground; a curious policy. If the objective is to have a crude oil reserve ready and quickly available in time of crisis, how much simpler and how much cheaper it would be to explore for and locate those oil deposits on national lands that the government offered to sell at bargain basement prices, drill the wells, cap them, and have them ready and available if and when they are needed. Why not?

It is a simple and straightforward option. It would avoid waste, hold down deficits, benefit society. Why, then, hasn't a single one of our distinguished senators demanded it from the Senate floor, or one of our economizing congressmen proposed it in the House, or any of our academic virtuosi paused from mathematical esoterica at least to raise the question, Why not?

The only answer I could elicit from the experts was that it would put government into the oil business. If in answer to their answer, I asked again: Why not? there would be only the stone face of taboo: the taboo of creeping socialism.

We have yet to confront the most crucial problem, that of survival when the fossil fuel is gone, when the well is finally empty. That we reserve for the chapter that follows.

Notes

1. Hotelling, Harold. ''The Economics of Exhaustible Resources.'' *Journal of Political Economy* 39, no. 2 (April 1931), pp. 137–175.

2. I plead to being the sole exception. My brief protest was lost in the sea of silence. Solo, Robert A. *Synthetic Rubber: A Case Study in Technological Development under Government Direction*, p. 126. Study no. 18 of the Subcommittee on Patents, Trademarks and Copyrights of the Committee of the Judiciary, U.S. Congress. Senate. Washington, DC: U.S. Government Printing Office, 1959.

3. Schmalensee, Richard. "Appropriate Governmental Policy towards Commercialization of New Energy Supply Technologies." *The Energy Journal* 1, no. 2 (April 1980).

20 • Survival

The Day of Reckoning

The message is simple. The message is clear. There is just so much, and not any more. What is taken out is gone for good. The oil wells of Venezuela, of Nigeria, of the North Sea, of the USSR, of Saudi Arabia, of Iran and Iraq, will also run dry. Just when is never certain. Unsuspected reserves will certainly be uncovered. New fields will be found. There will be blips in the curve of depletion. But necessarily, finally, the well will be empty.

How soon will the wells of the world run dry? In the February 1981 issue of *Science*, an article by Charles Hall and Cutler Cleveland reported a study by a team of Cornell scientists on trends in the cost of drilling for new oil. In that report, they specified what they called a "break-even point," where the cost in *energy* of obtaining new oil, that is, the energy that would be required to find and bring a barrel of oil from out of the earth, would be just equal to the energy that could be obtained from that barrel of oil; hence, where new drilling would cease to add anything to the currently available store of energy. They determined that in the United States we would arrive at this break-even point "in about twenty years if industry holds to its 1978 drilling rate . . . but if the rate continues to increase the break-even point would occur in the mid-1980s."[1]

Thirty, forty, fifty years: the beginning of the end is in sight. Our technology, the whole structure of our industry and society, is based on the availability of petroleum, a resource that is being rapidly depleted, with its end in sight. This poses a problem for the United States, for western capitalism, for the world.

We are left with the problem of survival. There is no satisfactory response to the question, How rapidly shall we allow the petroleum resource to be depleted? any more than there is to the poet's "shall the world end with a bang or a whimper?" They are indeed the same question: Should we sink gradually into deeper poverty or live it up until a total collapse? But our interest is not in when to die, but in how to survive. To survive means to develop an alternative, hopefully a benign and low-cost energy alternative. It follows as a criterion in a social policy of survival that we deplete at a rate not greater than the time needed to develop and make available a secure and acceptable energy alternative; with the development of that energy alternative as the responsibility of the state.

Energy Policy and the American State

The American's ingrained perception of government and its works is by no means entirely negative. Toward the public agencies and instruments of ideological nationalism (the military forces and the Department of State) and toward the public agencies and instruments of ideological liberalism (the judiciary as the shield of property and the arbiter of contract, necessary for the market's operation), American attitudes verge on the worshipful. It is where the economy is concerned, in that which relates to public initiative and control in the broad domain of production and distribution, that the myth of creeping socialism comes fully into play. No careers of high honor and responsibility are opened to the dedicated professional in the public service there. Borrowed businessmen, quick in-and-outers from the corporate executive suite, ex-admirals and ex-generals, rule every executive roost in the apparatus of governance. The problem with the borrowed businessman and with the former military officer is not one of ability or good will. It is that they have been shaped by their work and selected by their peers for capacities different than those needed for the tasks of the civil state. Their ingrained goals, criteria of choice, and knowledge of operations belong to another world of experience and achievement. They have not been attuned to the general interest or sensitized to the table of social values. And they bring into the apparatus of governance a fear of governance. An antistate bias and a contempt for the state's potential are built into the operation of the state.

The consequences of all this are predictable. Without continuity, the knowledge relevant to the formation of policy does not accumulate. Without a lifetime dedication, the competencies needed for the tasks of high governance do not develop. Closed off from access to the top, without the expectation or hope of high responsibility, the working body of the state lacks the capacity for initiative and innovation. The able and dedicated are weeded out of the professional ranks. Only the timid, who toady to their business betters, and the order of clerks remain. Inbred timidity burrows itself in red tape. How else can it shield itself from blame? The result is not wickedness, but weakness and incompetence and the general incapacity to comprehend and control social and technological phenomena. It could be no other way.

All this is reflected in the events, and explains the paradoxes, of atomic energy and the failures of the synfuel program, that is, of the public effort to develop an energy alternative to fossil fuels.

Atomic Energy

It cannot be said that the American state has not invested in the development of an energy alternative. From the 1950s through the late 1970s, it invested billions of dollars annually in the development of nuclear energy for civilian use. Nearly the whole of that funding was devoted to the development of water-cooled reactors.

The only possible rationale for the public investment in energy research and development is the desire to make available an energy alternative preferred because it is cheaper, and/or safer, and/or more secure than fossil fuel. From the beginning, it was clear that nuclear energy is dangerous. It is polluting. It generates great quantities of radioactive waste that will remain dangerous for thousands of years and for which no means of safe disposal has been devised. It derives from a resource that is depletable and has been rapidly depleted. It provides no portable form of energy that could substitute for gasoline in the automobile. And it is expensive. Under the most sanguine expectations, the water-cooled reactor would enable no substantial cost advantage over the use of fossil fuels. Yet for decades, the American government chose to invest its billions of dollars in this and in no other avenue of energy development. Nor did those in authority ever consider and weigh the possible payoffs in lowering costs or providing a safe, secure, and nonpolluting energy source from alternative avenues of energy development.

Now, nearly half a century after the program was launched, the establishment of nuclear installations is resisted and feared, and the nuclear operations already established stand as the great white elephants of the energy system. Why, then, have we had decades of public investment in nuclear research and development, with never a systematic and serious evaluation of alternatives?

The advent of nuclear energy was through an extraordinary conclave of scientific and engineering talent in the conditions of total war. It was developed in the secrecy and autonomy of the military establishment; and when called forth by President Eisenhower as purveyor of "atoms for peace," it emerged fully formed into the light of civilian visibility and nominal democratic control, already possessed of a network of powerful industrial clients, with great national laboratories at its disposal, and linked to the new nuclear physics it had implanted in the universities. Nowhere in the civil state did there exist an authority responsible for the general interest, sensitized to the table of social values, attuned to the national purpose, with the competence, independence, and power needed to consider, evaluate, and control the programs of the Atomic Energy Commission (AEC).

Even if such a locus of competence, responsibility, and power had existed, the same mistakes might have been made. But the absence of that authority made it absolutely certain that the powerful, narrowly focused atomic energy establishment would replicate itself generation after generation. Nuclear engineers who had designed and were interested in the development of the water-cooled reactor would recruit and train nuclear engineers interested in the further development of the water-cooled nuclear reactor, who would, in their turn, recruit and train nuclear engineers interested in the further development of water-cooled nuclear reactors, on and on. The atomic energy establishment would function but never transcend or offer a challenge to that function. It would advocate the doing of what it was geared up to do, doing what it knew how to do; doing that, seeking that, and nothing else; driving ahead full steam with rudder fixed, dragging society in its wake.

In a mode of thought ruled by the fallacy of creeping socialism, there could not develop, and there did not exist, anywhere in the civilian state a competence and power sensitive to and responsible for national priorities and the problems of the whole that could comprehend and control the activities of the AEC. Because the policy-making and control centers of the American political system were without the capacity to comprehend, evaluate, or exercise an independent judgment concerning the AEC, or to judge its direction, or to assess its potentials in comparison to alternatives, perforce the expertise of the AEC was entirely relied upon. For that reason, during those long decades the public invested only in the nuclear, concentrating on the water-cooled reactor, neglecting all the other avenues of energy development.

Synfuels

Driven to the wall by oil embargo, its vulnerability exposed, the American government started a program in the late 1970s to develop synthetic substitutes for petroleum. Given the weakness and timidity ingrained into the operation of a civil state that was shredded by the drive to privatize and ruled by the fallacy of creeping socialism, that program was from the start destined to failure and frustration.

The program eschewed any initiative or effort to develop the new synfuels through any public agency. For the development of new synthetic fuels it turned to private business enterprise. As in every other instance during post–World War II decades, when the American civil state sought to promote the development of technology in the private sector, it relied on two strategies, both perfectly adapted to incompetence, timidity, and a flight from responsibility by the agencies of government nominally in charge. These were the strategies of (1) scatter grants and (2) demonstrations. In both strategies, the administering bureaucracy invites proposals from businesses or individuals, usually academic scientists or research consultants, to do research on X, develop Y, or demonstrate Z. The proposals, once submitted, are passed through the sanctifying sieve of an advisory committee normally drawn from among the ranks of the grant or contract recipients. Certain proposals are chosen, and the grants or contracts are made accordingly. Known, if unpracticed, energy technologies were to be demonstrated, ranging from solar-heated homes to a massive installation intended to generate electricity through the interaction of the surface and the deep waters of the ocean, including solar collectors and concentrators, windmills, photovoltaic cells, and organic materials from fertilized ponds to be used as fuel or chemical feedstocks; always in the hope that following these demonstrations, someone would somehow want to do something about what was being demonstrated.

Grants to pay for the experimental development of new technologies were scattered among corporate and academic recipients. Experiment should be a step in learning. But learning requires, in effect, a brain, that is, a center for the accumulation, evaluation, and dissemination of the information that the experimenting produces, that probes the causes of failure, that discerns the potentials implicit in success, that weighs costs against benefits in choosing new directions, that identifies blind alleys, that eliminates the fraudulent, that accumulates experience and builds carefully on what has been learned as the base for new levels of searching. No such center for the evaluation and coordination of the grant-supported experiments scattered in academia and among the corporations existed, nor could any such center evolve in an American state ruled by the fallacy of creeping socialism. The program relied on the hope and faith that somehow, somewhere, out of the scattering of projects and the operation of free enterprise, somebody would make something good happen; making manifest the belief that if dollars are fed into its maw, an omni-competent market will do the rest.

Scatter grant and demonstration projects share these characteristics: They impose no responsibilities on the state. No planning, no organization, not even the monitoring of complex and purposeful activity, is required on the part of the state. Nor are the public agencies who establish the program, or the bureaucracy that administers it, or the advisory committees that sanction the grants or contracts, credited with its successes or answerable for its failures. Accountability is limited to the honest disposition of appropriated monies. There is no feedback of information in the system of demonstrations and scatter grants to guide the future formulation of policy, or even to guide choice in the selection of future demonstrators or experimenters.

Here is a public activity that poses no challenge to the omni-competent market, nor any threat of creeping socialism. It imposes no responsibility on anyone, has no clear objectives and no means to evaluate the performance of those in charge. It requires neither hard decisions, nor creative choice, nor foresightful planning, nor the exercise of any particular competence. A more perfect instrument could not be designed for timidity, incompetence, and irresponsibility in a denigrated, subordinated civil state formed under the fallacy of creeping socialism and administered by quick in-and-outers from the corporate executive suite. Although scatter grants and demonstration projects have been standard practice for half a century, I can find no evidence that either has ever resulted in any significant scientific or technological innovation or advance.

At the nadir of his popularity, seeking something that would capture the public imagination and enthusiasm, on July 29, 1979, President Carter proposed a $100 billion program to produce synthetic petroleum from coal. What strategies were to be pursued in this ambitious undertaking? Again, scatter grants and demonstrations! A new public Synthetic Fuels Corporation, stocked with authentic bankers and high-paid corporate executives, was allocated $88 billion to establish the new industry by passing out the cash to private enterprise.

Now it is all gone as with the wind. The Synthetic Fuel Corporation is defunct. Of a viable synthetic fuel industry remains not a trace. There are no footprints left by all the scatter grants and demonstration projects. The grant-eaters and demonstrators took their money, folded their tents, and left.

Nations

Yet another distorting mode of thought, perhaps the most dangerous, the most threatening to survival of all, has left its mark on the energy record. It is of ideas clustered around that of the nation, with its monopoly of righteousness, its brute prerogatives, its apartness, its collective egoism; this, in a world where all nations breathe the same air, excrete in the same sewer, drink from the same well, and where the flow of ideas and information defy the imposition of political boundaries.

It would matter not a whit to the cars on the road, to the warmth in the home, to that which drives the wheels of industry, whether it is Peter or Pytor or Pierre or Pedro who finds, invents, develops a more benign, more secure energy source and system. To find that source and system is a universal imperative in the face of a critical resource depletion.

Rationally, *public efforts* to deal with a world problem would be organized on a world scale, or at least transnationally, so as to tap the best available research capabilities, to avoid replication, and to share information. They are not. Certainly in the efforts to develop a fossil fuel alternative they were not. Invariably, public programs were organized national enclave by national enclave, without coordination, without cooperation, held apart by the fallacy of sovereign nationhood.

It is in the rational interest of every American that the homes of Western Europe be warmed by and its industries run on natural gas from Siberia, for otherwise, West European needs must overflow to press on and more rapidly deplete the fuel reserve on which we in the United States depend. For the same reason, it is in the rational interest of every American that the Chinese develop offshore petroleum supplies to satisfy their own needs and those of the Japanese. A rational American policy would welcome, promote, and facilitate such developments as these, for they delay the day of reckoning, when the reserves on which we depend are exhausted. In each instance, American policy sought exactly the opposite, risking the wrath of its allies in efforts to block the pipeline that would supply Western Europe with Siberian natural gas, and in the concerted effort to stop the sale and export of deep drilling equipment and technology to the Soviet Union or to the countries of the Socialist bloc.

Note

1. Hall, Charles and Cleveland, Cutler. "Petroleum Drilling and Production in the United States: Yield per Effort and Net Energy Analysis." *Science* 211, no. 4482 (6 February 1981), p. 579.

Index

Abernathy, William J., 84
AEC. *See* Atomic Energy Commission
Afghanistan
  U.S. intervention in, 4
Agency for Industrial Management
  (AIM), 42, 59–64, 92–94, 112
  anti-mergers, 89–90
  industrial development, 107–12, 122
  management of science information,
    106
  small enterprises, 91–92
Aggregate spending, 23, 31, 33, 35,
  37, 38, 142–43
Agriculture
  extension services, 95
  land grant colleges, 94–95
  and the neoclassical mode of
    thought, 12, 35
  policy, 94–96
  research centers, 95
AIM. *See* Agency for Industrial
  Management
Albania
  communism in, 5–6
Angola
  U.S. intervention in, 4
Anti-inflation policy, 16
Antitrust law, 84, 90
Arabia, 174, 184, 185
Argentina, 165
Armenia
  communism in, 5–6
Army Corps of Engineers, 97*n. 12*
Atomic Energy Commission (AEC),
  120, 194–95
Australia, 72*n. 1*, 109

Balance of trade, 131–32. *See also*
  International trade
Bank of Japan, 52
Banks
  American banking system, 38
  commercial, 24
  development, 92–93, 112
Belgium, 71*n. 1*
Black Monday, 27
Bonds, 26–27, 34
Boulding, Kenneth, 179–80
Bretton Woods, 119, 137
Budget policy, 24
Bulgaria
  communism in, 5–6
Bush, President George, 4–5, 6

Canada, 72*n. 1*
Capitalism, 3
  Marx's predictions, 11
  post–World War II, 15
  Western, 19, 191
Cartels *(keiretsu)*, 52, 94
Carter, President Jimmy, 16, 24–25
  energy policy, 187–88, 197
  international trade policy, 148
  laissez-faire policies, 39
  welfare policies, 16
Cash balances, 147–52
Central Intelligence Agency (CIA), 3,
  5, 18, 115
China
  communism, 115, 179
  energy, 198
  laissez-faire policies, 16
  war with Japan, 50

CIA. *See* Central Intelligence Agency
Clark, Kim B., 84
Cleveland, Cutler, 191
Cold war, 5, 120
Collective bargaining, 81
Common Market. *See* European
    Common Market
Communism, 3–4, 18, 115, 179
    threat to United States, 5–6
Conglomeration, 84–90
Congress
    and public policy, 59, 61, 116–21
    role in energy, 185
    role in taxes, 25, 36–37
Consumers
    credit, 30
    effect of OPEC on, 186–87
    saving, 14–15
Consumption expenditure, 30
Cooperative research associations, 94
Corporations
    as cause of stagflation, 38–39
    industrial policies, 42, 82
    management of industrial sector, 62–63
    price and wage policies, 20–21
    during recession, 16
    taxes, 70
Currency, 138, 141–45

DARPA. *See* Defense Advanced
    Research Projects Agency
Defense
    U. S. military expenditures, 33,
        113–15
Defense Advanced Research Projects
    Agency (DARPA), 62
Deficit finance, 25, 33
Deflation, 35, 137
Demilitarization, 4–5
Denmark, 71n. 1
Department of Health, Education, and
    Welfare (HEW), 105
Depression, 10–40, 177, 179. *See also*
    Employment; Inflation;
    Unemployment
    and the welfare state, 11–12
Devaluation, 136–37
Disarmament, 4–5, 7, 66
Distributional justice, 39–40

Eastern Europe. *See individual
    countries*
ECM. *See* European Common Market
Economics
    macro, 14, 19
    micro, 14, 19
    recovery, 17
    reforms, 42–58
    research and development, 77–78,
        196–97
Education
    in Japan, 45–46
    research and development, 75,
        77–78, 196–97
    technological advances, 99–107
    in the United States, 74, 83
EEC. *See* European Economic
    Community
Egypt
    subventions to, 4
Eisenhower, President Dwight,
    184–85, 194
El Salvador
    subventions to, 4–5, 115
Employment. *See also* Depression;
    Inflation; Unemployment
    during the Carter administration, 16
    Keynesian views, 13–14
    and price stability, 9–40, 63
    work force, 169–70
Energy. *See* Natural resources;
    Synfuels
England. *See* Great Britain
European Common Market (ECM),
    154, 155–57
European Economic Community
    (EEC), 115, 154, 155–57
Exchange rates, 138, 141–42
Expenditure management, 29, 32–40
    deficit financing, 34–35
    interest-free, 36–38
    non-diversionary spending, 25,
        33–34, 36
    practices, 32
    and public debt, 35–37

FBI. *See* Federal Bureau of
    Investigation
Federal Bureau of Investigation (FBI), 60

Federal Reserve Board, 13, 17, 23–24, 27, 30, 36, 37, 60, 96, 110, 111, 148–50
Federal Trade Commission, 84, 90
Finland, 71*n. 1*
Fiscal policy, 24, 30–31
France
cooperative research associations, 94
expenditure management, 32
gross national product, 71*n. 1*
industrial revolution, 101
laissez-faire policies, 16
military spending, 124
productivity, 71*n. 1*
unemployment, 71*n. 1*
French Indicative Planning Authority, 32, 63
Fulbright, Senator, 144

George, Henry, 96
George, Lloyd, 144, 145
Germany
British investment in, 165
cooperative research associations, 94
distribution of income, 72*n. 1*
gross national product, 71*n. 1*
hauptschule, 67, 101–2
industrial revolution, 101
international trade, 144–45
laissez-faire policies, 16
merging of East and West, 6, 115
militarism, 6
military spending, 113, 124
Nazi war machine, 3–4, 6
productivity, 71*n. 1*
unemployment, 71*n. 1*
GI Bill of Rights, 119
GNP. *See* Gross national product
Gorbachev, Mikhail, 3–8, 115
Great Britain, 13. *See also* United Kingdom
economy, 165
education, 99–100
exchange rates, 138
industrial revolution, 101
international trade, 135–36, 144–45, 165
laissez-faire policies, 16
socialism, 178–79

Great Depression, 11, 13, 16, 19, 21, 50–51, 89, 137, 151
Gross national product (GNP), 26
and international trade, 142–43, 163
U.S. compared with other countries', 71*n. 1*

Haiti, 164
Hall, Charles, 191
HEW. *See* Department of Health, Education, and Welfare
Hitler, Adolf, 6
Holloman, Herbert, 114–15, 122
Honduras, 164
Hong Kong, 138
Hotelling, Harold, 182
Hungary
communism in, 5–6

IMF. *See* International Monetary Fund
Imports, 169
Income
distribution, 69, 71–72*n. 1*
per capita, 26
India, 169
Industry
corporate policies, 82
development, 42
financing, 107–12
in Japan *(zaibatsu),* 49, 50, 51, 52, 108
management, 42, 62–63, 79–92
productivity, 65–125
Industry Rationalization Council (Japan), 51
Inflation, 9–40, 177. *See also* Depression; Employment; Unemployment
acceptable level, 33
anti-inflation policy, 16
monetary policy, 22–25, 110–11
during the 1970s, 15–16
policy-based, 22
Interest rates, 16
manipulation, 24–25
International Monetary Fund (IMF), 7
International trade, 127–71, 177, 179
American securities, 150
benefits, 129–33, 157, 159–62
economics of, 168

International trade *(continued)*
exchange rates, 138
and the money market, 148
policies, 129–33, 163–71
balance of trade, 131–32
mercantilism, 129–31
systems
evaluation, 139
history, 135–38
imbalance, 139–40
trade blocs, 159, 161–62, 166–67
Iran
energy, 191
subventions to, 4
Iraq, 191
Israel
subventions to, 4, 115
Italy
distribution of income, 72n. 1
productivity, 71n. 1
unemployment, 71n. 1

Japan, 39. *See also* Ministry of
Agriculture and Commerce;
Ministry of Commerce and
Industry; Ministry of
International Trade and Industry
banking, 92
Board of Trade, 51
culture, 45
distribution of income, 72n. 1
economy, 49
educational system, 45–46, 101
energy, 198
exchange rates, 138
gross national product, 71n. 1
history, 43–45, 48, 49–52
imports, 169
industrial development, 43–45, 52,
53, 108
industrial groups *(zaibatsu),* 49, 50,
51, 52
international trade, 145, 171
military expenditure, 113
Ministry of Agriculture and Forestry,
49
Ministry of Finance, 47, 50
Ministry of Munitions (MM), 50–51
per capita growth rate, 72n. 1

Japan *(continued)*
postwar restructuring, 51–52
productivity, 71n. 1
public policy, 54–55
unemployment, 71n. 1
U.S. occupation, 51
Japanese Development Bank, 52
Japanese Diet, 47–48
Japanese External Trade Association, 51
Japanese External Trade Organization,
51–52
Johnson, Chalmer, 43

Kantrow, Alan M., 84
Kennedy administration, 60
Keynes, John Maynard, 13, 14–15, 22,
132, 144
Keynesian policies, 19, 22, 24
deficit financing, 34–35
and expenditure management, 32–33
full employment, 10, 11, 13–14
golden age, 15
and international trade, 142–43
during the 1970s, 15
non-diversionary spending, 33–34, 36
price stability, 11
and stagflation, 38–39
Khmer Rouge
U.S. support, 4
Khrushchev, Nikita, 115
Korea
U. S. investment in, 164
war, 4
Korekiyo, Takakashi, 50

Labor, 30. *See also* Trade unions
collective bargaining, 81
shortage, 119
training, 102–3
work force, 169–70
Laissez-faire policies, 16, 97n. 12
agricultural, 94
during the Carter administration, 39
Land grant colleges, 94–95
Latin America
dictatorship, 4
Line of credit
interest-free, 36–37
Luxembourg, 71n. 1

MAC. *See* Ministry of Agriculture and Commerce
Malthus, Thomas, 131
Manchuria, 50
Manhattan Project, 120
Marshall Plan, 119, 145
Marx, Karl, 11, 83, 96–97*n. 2*
MCI. *See* Ministry of Commerce and Industry
Meiji restoration, 49
Melman, Seymour, 86, 114
Mercantilism, 129–31
Mergers, 84–90, 157
Mexico, 164
Militarism
  in Germany, 6
Military
  U. S. defense expenditures, 33, 113–15
Ministry of Agriculture and Commerce (MAC), 49. *See also* Ministry of Agriculture and Forestry; Ministry of Commerce and Industry
Ministry of Agriculture and Forestry (Japan), 49
Ministry of Commerce and Industry (MCI) (Japan), 49
Ministry of Finance (Japan), 47, 50
Ministry of International Trade and Industry (MITI), 39, 42, 43–58
  characteristics of success, 54–55
  education and training, 45–46
  Higher-Level Public Officials Examination, 46
  history, 45–46
  industrial development, 108–9
  Laws and Ordinances Examination Committee, 47
  policy formation and implementation, 47–48
  postwar restructuring, 51–52
  promotion and retirement, 46–47
  as role model for the United States, 60–62
Ministry of Munitions (MM), 50–51
MITI. *See* Ministry of International Trade and Industry
MM. *See* Ministry of Munitions

Monetary policy, 13, 23–24, 30–31, 110–11

NASA. *See* National Aeronautics and Space Administration
National Aeronautics and Space Administration (NASA), 105, 120–21
Nationalism, 6
NATO, 5, 6, 18, 115
Natural resources, 173–98. *See also* Synfuels
  and Congress, 185
  depletion, 181–86
  energy, 179, 191, 193–95
  oil, 174, 182, 186–87
  pollution, 122, 193–95
  protection, 7
Neoclassical mode of thought, 12–13, 70, 144, 174
  in agricultural markets, 12
  decline in aggregate demand, 12
  in Japan, 44
Netherlands, The, 71*n. 1*
  Bouwcentrum, 94
New Deal, 60, 89, 95, 97*n. 12*
New York Times, 62
Nicaragua
  demilitarization, 5
  financing of contras in, 4
Nigeria, 191
Nixon, President Richard, 39, 121, 185
Non-diversionary expenditure, 25, 33–34, 36
Norway, 71*n. 1*

OPEC
  effect on stagflation, 15–16, 183
  during the 1970s, 22
  prices and effect on consumers, 186–87

Pakistan
  subventions to, 4, 115
Pangloss, Dr., 11
Peace Corps, 60
Pentagon, 62, 93, 104, 105, 113–15
Per capita income, 26
Pol Pot
  U.S. support, 4

Price stability, 29
  fixity, 20
  and full employment, 9–40, 63
  and OPEC prices, 186–87
  during stagflation, 19–20
Price/wage policy, 39, 63–64
Productivity, 40, 65–125, 177
  rise in, during the 1950s and 1960s,
    21–22
  post–World War II, 70, 72n. 1
  statistics, 71n. 1
Profits, 27, 164
Public policy, 73–74
Pundits, 27

Reagan, President Ronald, 16, 24–25,
    39, 110, 121, 148, 185
Recession
  deficit financing, 34–35
  effect on social programs, 19
  during the 1980s, 33, 116–17, 138
  recovery, 16–17, 30–31
Republican party, 33
Research and development (R&D)
  disarmament activities, 7–8
  education, 75, 77–78, 196–97
  funding, 70
Ricardo, David, 129
Romania
  communism in, 5–6
Roosevelt, President Franklin, 39, 89,
    95, 97n. 12
Rural Electrification Administration,
    97n. 12

Salaries, 27
Saudi Arabia, 191
Schlesinger, James, 187–88
Schumpeter, Joseph, 73
Science
  education and training, 103–7
  research and development, 196–97
Securities and Exchange Commission
    (SEC), 89
Smith, Adam, 79, 96n. 1, 129, 160
Socialism, 175
  elimination, 16
  spread, 178–79
Sovereign individualism, 178

Soviet Union, 18
  communism, 3–4, 115
  disarmament, 7, 66
  energy policy, 191, 198
  military spending, 124–25
Spain
  distribution of income, 72n. 1
Stagflation, 19–22, 29, 177, 179
  cause, 38–39
  effect of OPEC on, 15–16
  during the 1970s, 15–16, 183
Stock market
  crash of 1987, 27
Supreme Court (of the United States),
    8
Sweden
  distribution of income, 72n. 1
  gross national product, 71n. 1
  unemployment, 71n. 1
Switzerland, 71n. 1, 138
Synfuels, 195–97. See also Natural
    resources

Taiwan, 164
Taxes, 34
  and aggregate expenditure, 23
  concessions, 33
  and Congress, 25, 36–37
  corporate, 70
  and international trade, 143–45
Taylor, Frederick Winslow, 79–82
Technology, 40, 65–125
  decline in U.S., 66, 177
  education, 74–75, 99–107
  research and development,
    196–97
  transfer, 166–67
Tennessee Valley Authority, 97n. 12
Thatcher, Margaret, 6
Third World countries, 170–71,
    183–84
Tokyo Imperial University, 45–46
Tokyo Law School, 49
Tokyo School of Law, 46
Trade unions, 16, 21. See also Labor
  as cause of stagflation, 38–39
  collective bargaining, 81
TVA. See Tennessee Valley
    Authority

Unemployment, 9–40, 179. *See also* Depression; Employment; Inflation
and deficit financing, 25
during the 1970s, 15–16
post–World War II, 15, 71–72n. 1
during stagflation, 38
statistics, 71n. 1
United Kingdom. *See also* Great Britain
cooperative research associations, 94
distribution of income, 72n. 1
gross national product, 71n. 1
productivity, 71n. 1
unemployment, 71n. 1
United States
banking system, 38
borrowing, 33
demilitarization, 4–5
democracy, 3
disarmament, 4–5, 7
distribution of income, 71–72n. 1
economic policy, 155
education, 74, 83
energy policy, 188–89, 192–95
exchange rates, 138
gross national product, 71n. 1
imports, 169
industrial management, 79–92
industrial revolution, 101
international trade, 127–71
military spending, 3, 6, 17, 33, 113–15
national debt, 17, 26
occupation of Japan, 51
productivity, 65–125
decline, 66, 177

United States *(continued)*
productivity *(continued)*
statistics, 71n. 1
public debt, 26–27
public policy, 59, 73–74
security, 3–4
socialism, 178–79
technological development, 69–70
unemployment, 71n. 1
U. S. Department of Agriculture, 105
U. S. Department of Energy, 105
U. S. Department of Justice, 84, 90
U. S. Department of State, 3, 159, 192
U. S. Supreme Court, 84
U. S. Treasury, 30, 36, 38, 148

Veblen, Thorstein, 83–84, 88
Venezuela, 191
Vietnam war, 4

Wages, 27, 63–64
price freeze, 39
during stagflation, 19–20
Wall Street, 27, 67, 111–12
Warsaw Pact, 4, 18, 115
Watt, James, 185
Webb, Jim, 121
Welfare policies
under the Carter administration, 16
under the Reagan administration, 16
Work force, 169–70
World Bank, 7
World War I, 6, 69
World War II, 15, 49, 72n. 1, 80, 84, 102, 119, 137, 144, 159, 165, 195

Yawata Steel Company (Japan), 49
Yoshino-Kishi, 50

About the Author

Robert A. Solo, Professor of Economics Emeritus at Michigan State, has degrees from both Harvard and Cornell. His career spans teaching and research in economics, as well as work on Roosevelt's New Deal, Puerto Rico's Fomento, the OECD, and NASA. Professor Solo's publications include novels, television documentaries, journal articles, and numerous books in economics.